Praise for *A Gentle*

"It's cliché now to say that our society is polarized, but the solutions are not much in evidence. This book proposes practicing Proverbs 15:1: 'A gentle answer turns away wrath.' But Scott is not putting forth some mere technique. He shows that we will never be gentle and kind with one another unless we receive the perfect gentleness of gospel grace that restructures our hearts and identities so we can speak the truth in love to others. A great, highly practical volume that points us to the tenderness of Jesus: 'a bruised reed he will not break.'"

—Tim Keller, pastor emeritus of Redeemer Presbyterian Church in New York City

"Wow! What a great book. Endorsements are limited to two to three sentences. Yet, I need two to three pages to adequately celebrate this book. It is timely, surgically precise, convicting, and encouraging. We will be better humans because of it."

—Max Lucado, bestselling author and pastor of Oak Hills Church in San Antonio, Texas

"Scott Sauls is the preeminent voice for fractured, polarized times. No voice speaks with such fresh hope, clarifying wisdom, and rooted orthodoxy—all from a posture of unifying grace. Because he actually, genuinely, lives what he espouses, Scott's every word is read under our roof. Very few pastors or theologians have more spiritually formed our family than his. And very few books could change the conversation around our office watering holes, our family dinner tables, and across our aisles and fences across the globe like this one."

—Ann Voskamp, bestselling author of *One Thousand Gifts* and *The Broken Way*

"For all the years I've known Scott, he's been a resource for how to navigate difficult conversations. Why? Because this message is who *he* is. This book could not have come at a better time, as we navigate a culture of polarization. I'm challenged and reminded of who Jesus is, and who I aim to be—gentle and lowly in heart. This is a heart-changing book!"

—Rebekah Lyons, bestselling author of *Rhythms of Renewal* and *You Are Free*

"I love *A Gentle Answer* for three reasons. First, as a beaten-down and discouraged young pastor—who was ready to run—the whole trajectory of my life and ministry was changed by a single sentence spoken to me by a gentle-hearted man. Second, this book is a wonderful example of its own topic, it powerfully exposes and confronts us, while being beautifully gentle and encouraging at the same time. Third, in a culture that glories in outrage, I can't think of a more needed and timelier book than this one and I don't know of anyone who wouldn't benefit from reading it regularly, including me."

—Dr. Paul David Tripp, pastor, speaker, and bestselling author of *New Morning Mercies*

"In a culture where being Christian doesn't necessarily mean being Christlike, *A Gentle Answer* reorients our hearts to the ways of Jesus. With the humility of a fellow student and the kindness of a trusted friend, our pastor, Scott Sauls, examines nuanced issues of anger, forgiveness, and criticism in the clarifying light of the gospel. This book is both enlightening and challenging but above all, it is an invitation to know Jesus more deeply and love others the way he does."

—Amanda Bible Williams and Raechel Myers, founders of She Reads Truth

"In his inimitable prose, Scott has once again beautifully reminded us about the upside nature of Christ's kingdom; that is, regardless of our pedigree or position, our gentle grace-filled answers possess power—the power to heal, inspire, and transform. What we often fail to realize is that kindness leads to repentance, grace leads to redemption. I will be turning to this book again and again, where Scott points me to the gentle grace of Jesus, full of grace and truth, as the model, motivation, and empowerment of the (hopefully!) generous spirit and speech we all need to have in the midst of life's brokenness."

—Dr. Julius J. Kim, president of The Gospel Coalition

"Scott Sauls is someone who has his priorities in the right place. In a culture that seems to reward bombast and bloviation, *A Gentle Answer* offers a different way. Scott understands that we need to care for one another's souls when we enter into difficult conversations. What an example Scott gives of a gentle way we can follow that reflects a Christian's confidence that Jesus is in control."

—Michael Wear, author of *Reclaiming Hope*

"Gentleness is not compromise. It's not a soft, mushy posture. To be gentle in a culture of outrage is rather a radical, dangerous, costly choice—but one with the potential to actually break the vicious cycles that destroy us. With *A Gentle Answer*, Scott Sauls offers Christians a gentle—in the strongest sense of the word—nudge to return to the Jesus way of responding to a world full of things to (rightfully) be outraged about. It's a much better way, and this timely book shows why."

—Brett McCracken, senior editor at The Gospel Coalition and author of *Uncomfortable*

"While we all seem to recognize the need for gracious, civil discourse today, few people have practical suggestions for how we can change. *A Gentle Answer* gives us a biblical, compelling model for speaking in a conflicted and antagonistic society."

—Alan Noble, PhD, editor-in-chief of *Christ and Pop Culture* and author of *Disruptive Witness*

"The rights and privileges that I experience today as a black man were secured for me by a movement whose locus of power was in their response: Nonviolent. Peaceful. Gentle. In an historic irony, gentleness toppled Jim Crow, and literally changed the face of our democracy. Decades removed from these legislative gains, Scott Sauls reminds us of the essential and needed attribute of gentleness in a world steeped in outrage and cancel culture."

—Dr. Bryan Loritts, executive pastor of Summit Church and author of *The Dad Difference*

"Outrage has become our national sport—anger the highest of our civic virtues. But as Scott Sauls persuades, the scandalous, gracious, lavish love of God calls his people to a better way. This is an urgent book for our fractured times, calling us to rigorous self-examination and to the gentle way of Jesus. Sauls is just the kind of voice we need in evangelicalism today."

—Jen Pollock Michel, award-winning author of *Surprised by Paradox* and *Keeping Place*

"Some books are really good on the merit of the writing alone. Other books aren't as well written but are prophetic. A few books rise to the surface, deserving the affirmation, 'so timely.' *A Gentle Answer* is a combination of all three. This was one of the easiest and most unsettling books to read. At times I'm nicer than I am gentle. This book calls for a bold love I want to grow more into. In a culture of mean-spirited diatribe, Scott Sauls invites us to consider just how subversive Jesus' command in Matthew 11:29 really is, 'Learn from me, for I am gentle and lowly in heart.' A gentle answer isn't a pragmatic tool for defusing an aggressor's anger. It's an indication that the grace and love of Jesus are gentling our hearts—that his kingdom has come near. So much so that we can risk leading with kindness, not rightness; listen more, launch less; confirm less prejudices and win more friends."

—Scotty Ward Smith, pastor emeritus of Christ Community Church and teacher in residence at West End Community Church

"Everyone has a 'them'—those whose views we don't want to tolerate. In Scott's signature style, he helps us see our own brokenness in this standoff culture with Jesus as the solution. In our secular feel-good world, words like *love* and *confront* can seem in opposition. Sauls helps us see how Jesus connects the two through a gentleness that is also bold. As we head into a polarizing election year, Sauls confronts us in a disturbing, necessary fashion with the way of Jesus."

—Missy Wallace, vice president and executive director of Global Faith & Work Initiative at Redeemer City to City

A GENTLE ANSWER

Also by Scott Sauls

Jesus Outside the Lines

Befriend

From Weakness to Strength

Irresistible Faith

A GENTLE ANSWER

OUR "SECRET WEAPON" in an AGE OF US AGAINST THEM

SCOTT SAULS

An Imprint of Thomas Nelson

Published in Nashville, Tennessee, by Nelson Books, an imprint of Thomas Nelson. Nelson Books and Thomas Nelson are registered trademarks of HarperCollins Christian Publishing, Inc.

Thomas Nelson titles may be purchased in bulk for educational, business, fund-raising, or sales promotional use. For information, please email SpecialMarkets@ThomasNelson.com.

ISBN 978-1-4002-1656-7 (eBook)
ISBN 978-1-4002-1655-0 (TP)

Library of Congress Cataloging-in-Publication Data

Names: Sauls, Scott, 1968- author.
Title: A gentle answer : our "secret weapon" in an age of us against them / Scott Sauls.
Description: Nashville, Tennessee : Nelson Books, 2020. | Includes bibliographical references. | Summary: "A remarkable vision for how Christians can live with countercultural gentleness in a perpetually angry, attacking, outraged time"-- Provided by publisher.
Identifiers: LCCN 2019049753 (print) | LCCN 2019049754 (ebook) | ISBN 9781400216550 (paperback) | ISBN 9781400216567 (ebook)
Subjects: LCSH: Kindness--Religious aspects--Christianity. | Christianity and culture.
Classification: LCC BV4647.K5 S28 2020 (print) | LCC BV4647.K5 (ebook) | DDC 261--dc23
LC record available at https://lccn.loc.gov/2019049753
LC ebook record available at https://lccn.loc.gov/2019049754

Printed in the United States of America

20 21 22 23 24 LSC 10 9 8 7 6 5 4 3

To Patti:
My partner in life and a fierce, gentle soul.

A gentle answer turns away wrath.

—Proverbs 15:1 NIV

Contents

Foreword

by Ray Ortlund

One of Christianity's most brilliant theologians, Jonathan Edwards, taught us that gentleness—he called it "a lamblike, dove-like spirit"—is not an optional extra but instead is "*the* true and distinguishing disposition of the hearts of Christians." In other words, gentleness is the most Christian way we can be.

I wonder what we think of that. Certainly, none of us oppose gentleness. But do we esteem gentleness? Have we moved all our chips onto the gentleness square, as if our very future depends on how gentle we prove to be? To the degree that we have renounced pushiness and embraced gentleness, we are making the real Jesus visible in our world today—which *is* success, no matter what else might happen to us.

Jesus himself said, "I am gentle and lowly in heart" (Matt. 11:29). And here is why that's amazing. We know a lot about Jesus, because he told us a lot about himself. We know about his beliefs and convictions, his mission and miracles, his death and resurrection and second coming. But the one and only time he opened up his chest—so to speak, to reveal his heart, his core being, who he is and always will be way down deep—how did

Jesus describe his deepest self? "Gentle and lowly." Therefore, gentleness isn't a strategy he resorts to now and then. It isn't one card he can lay down on the table. Gentleness is just who he is at the most profound level of his being. Here, then, is what we would never believe if Jesus hadn't told us. We have parachuted into a universe where *gentleness* is the ultimate reality—now and forever. No wonder that the true followers of Jesus stand out for their gentleness.

That is why I welcome *A Gentle Answer* by my friend, Scott Sauls. But not everyone will welcome this book. On both the right and the left, some will perceive Scott's book as threatening. In a way, I hope they do see it that way, because it is. *A Gentle Answer* does undermine all swagger-driven, domineering, win-at-all-costs, sub-Christian "Christianity," of every stripe and tribe. Scott's message is clear. Jesus himself sets the tone for everyone who wants to stop using him and start following him. If, like me, you refuse to be recruited for extremist agendas on both sides of the political and cultural divide, if you long for a path forward marked by the beauty of Jesus himself, then you can welcome *A Gentle Answer*. It will not let you down.

Both Scott and I are pastors in Nashville, Tennessee. We both pray for the power of the gospel to wash over our city with a gentle wave of healing, as never before. We both understand that, even as the Spirit descended on Jesus in the form of a dove (Matt. 3:16), the Spirit will descend on our city today not in the form of political power or moral superiority or doctrinal perfection but in the form of Christian gentleness. We both look for the day when the top news story in town is us Christians, starting with us pastors, befriending and embracing, confessing and forgiving, believing and rejoicing again. We both long for the day when all of us fed-up, and at times cynical, Christians are finally "leaping like calves from the stall" (Mal. 4:2), and gently offering that newness of life to others around. If there is any other way to get there, any strategy that leaves tenderness and humility and honesty and risk and reconciliation out of the equation, we would have found it by now. We've tried everything else. So, only Jesus remains. And he is reaching out to us today, offering himself afresh.

And one significant way he is reaching out to us is through Scott's new book, *A Gentle Answer.* As you read, may our Lord himself draw near.

Ray Ortlund,
Renewal Ministries, Nashville

Introduction

"*This generation is the first to* turn hate into an asset."

When Dr. John Perkins, the eighty-nine-year-old Christian minister and civil rights icon/activist, said these words at a recent leaders' gathering in Nashville, things I've been feeling about the current state of Western society came into sharper focus. For many years now, I've grown increasingly perplexed over what feels like a culture of suspicion, mistrust, and us-against-them. Whatever the subject may be—politics, sexuality, immigration, income gaps, women's concerns, race, or any other social matters over which people have differences—angst, suspicion, outrage, and outright hate increasingly shape our response to the world around us.

John Perkins knows suffering. His mother died when he was a baby. His father abandoned him when he was a child. His brother was killed during an altercation with a Mississippi police officer. As a black man during the civil rights era, he endured beatings and imprisonments and death threats. Since that time, Perkins has faithfully confronted injustice, racism, oppression, and violence while also advocating valiantly for reconciliation, peace, equality, healing, and hope.

If anyone has a right to be bitter, if anyone has a right to turn hate into an asset and use it to his own advantage, it is John Perkins. Yet instead of feeding the cycle of resentment and retaliation, he spends his life preaching against these wrongs while advocating for forgiveness and moving toward enemies in love. With the moral authority of one who practices what he preaches, Perkins's life is a sermon that heralds reconciliation and peace between divided people groups. He has built his life upon the belief that his Lord and Savior, Jesus Christ, has left no option except to advance neighbor-love through the tearing down of what scripture calls "dividing walls of hostility." This is an essential task for those who identify as followers of Jesus Christ, who laid down his life not only for his friends but also for his enemies. Jesus is a God of reconciliation and peace, not a God of hate or division or us-against-them (Eph. 2:14–22). He is the God of the gentle answer.

While some do not understand what it feels like to be ostracized, belittled, or persecuted, Dr. Perkins reminds us all that every person bears the image of God and is a carrier of the divine imprint. Because of this, every person is also entitled to being treated with honor, dignity, and respect. The inherent dignity of personhood makes the prophet's description of neighbor-love that much more essential in our dealings with one another: "He has told you, O man, what is good; and what does the Lord require of you but to do justice, and to love kindness" as an overflow of walking humbly with our God (Micah 6:8).

Hurtful behaviors such as violence, scorn, gossip, and slander injure both victim and perpetrator. The hurtful behavior certainly devastates its target, but the hate that lies beneath eats the haters alive, clouding their thinking, crippling their hearts, and diminishing their souls. In the end, those who injure become as miserable as those whom they injure. Those who vandalize someone else's body, spirit, or good name also vandalize themselves.

Those who yearn to do justice, love mercy, and walk humbly with their God advance righteousness by speaking and living a message of love—not a sappy, sentimental love, but one that is undergirded with truth and with the courage and wisdom needed to confront. Injured parties and their advocates must rise up with a prophetic voice that confronts the status quo when necessary. The prophetic voice comes from a righteous, Holy Spirit–filled anger that causes Christ's ambassadors to rise up in the name of love and say, "No more!"

While rising up to advance righteousness, God's people must also engage the inner battle to "sin not" in their anger (Ps. 4:4; Eph. 4:26). On the one hand, anger can serve as an instrument of true peace. Such righteous anger can be necessary and constructive. Many of the world's most important human-rights initiatives—abolishing the slave trade, confronting sex trafficking, initiating the #MeToo and #ChurchToo movements that expose abuse of power, opposing Hitler, advancing civil rights, and more—have harnessed the energy of righteous anger. These movements began because a person or group of people went public with their collective, righteous anger.

On the other hand, if we are not careful, anger that starts out as righteous can become unrighteous, injurious, and counterproductive to the name and cause of Jesus Christ. As Bono, the front man for the rock band U2, once said in a concert, "We must be careful in our efforts to confront the monster not to ourselves *become* the monster." Followers of Christ must especially concern themselves with using their anger for good, while also ensuring that no "root of bitterness" springs up in such a way that it causes trouble and defiles many (Heb. 12:15). While true faith is filled with holy fire, it is a fire that is meant for refining and healing, as opposed to dividing and destroying. If our faith ignites hurt rather than healing upon the bodies, hearts, and souls of other people—even those who treat us unkindly—then something has gone terribly wrong with our faith.

Perhaps for this reason, the Bible is careful to warn that all anger, including the constructive righteous kind, should be arrived at slowly and not from a reactive hair trigger. "Let every person be quick to hear, slow to speak, slow to anger;" the apostle James writes, "for the anger of man does not produce the righteousness of God. Therefore put away all filthiness and rampant wickedness and receive with meekness the implanted word, which is able to save your souls" (James 1:19–21). In being slow to anger through a spirit of meekness, we express the image of God in us, who, being both perfectly righteous and the universe's chief offended party, "forgives all [our] iniquity" and "crowns [us] with steadfast love and mercy" and "is merciful and gracious, *slow to anger* and abounding in steadfast love" (Ps. 103:3–4, 8, emphasis mine). If God's default response to human offense is to be *slow* in his anger—even the righteous kind—how much more should this be true of us, even when expressions of righteous anger may be entirely justified?

Jesus renounced outrage and advanced the power of a gentle answer throughout his ministry. In one instance, as they were traveling through a Samaritan village, Jesus' disciples were met with rejection, hostility, and scorn. Feeling offended and incensed by the Samaritans' inhospitable posture and disregard for their Lord, the disciples James and John, the so-called Sons of Thunder (due to their confrontational nature), suggested that Jesus retaliate by calling down fire from heaven to consume them. Jesus responded to the two brothers by rebuking them (Luke 9:51–59).

John Perkins's response to the injuries perpetrated toward him and other people of color honors our Lord in ways that the Sons of Thunder did not. Rather than calling down fire on his enemies, Perkins concluded that the best and only way to conquer outrage was with what he called a love that trumps hate. "Yielding to God's will can be hard," Perkins wrote in 1976. "And sometimes, it really hurts. But it always brings peace . . . You have to be a bit of a dreamer to imagine a world where love trumps hate—but I don't think being a dreamer is all that bad . . . I'm an old man, and this is one of my dreams: that my descendants will one day live in a land where people are quick to confess their wrongdoing and forgive the wrongdoing of others and are eager to build something beautiful together."[1]

Building something beautiful together will require participation from all sides. To those who are prone to injure, the call is to repent and to engage in the noble work of renouncing hatred and exercising love. To those who are vulnerable to becoming injured, the call is to participate in the noble work of resisting bitter and retaliating roots of anger while embracing truth-telling, advocacy, and forgiveness. To all of us, the universal call is to lay down our swords, listen, learn from our differences, and build something beautiful.

OUTRAGE AND ITS BROAD APPEAL

In 2014, *Slate* magazine released a series of essays collectively called "The Year of Outrage" and described, "From righteous fury to faux indignation, everything we got mad about . . . and how outrage has taken over our lives." Essay titles included "The Outrage Project," "The Life Cycle of Outrage," "What 'Outrage' Means," "Identity Outrage," "The Cultural Outrage Audit," "The Year in Liberal Outrage," "The Year in Conservative Outrage," "My Viral Outrage Hit," "Righteous Outrage," and "How Outrage Changed My Life."[2]

It seems there are as many things to get upset about as there are things to talk about.

In our current cultural moment, outrage has become more expected than surprising, more normative than odd, more encouraged than discouraged, more rewarded than rejected. Outrage undergirds each day's breaking news. It is part of the air that we breathe—a native language, a sick helping of emotional food and drink to satisfy our hunger for taking offense, shaming, and punishing. Outrage has become something we can't get away from, partly because we don't seem to *want* to get away from it. Instead of getting rid of all bitterness, rage, and anger as scripture urges us to do (Eph. 4:31), we form entire communities around our irritations and our hatreds. Tribes and echo chambers form, social media feeds grow, political pontifications multiply, book deals prosper, podcasts rant, and churches split. On some level, we are all engaged in the seemingly insatiable, ubiquitous theme of us-against-them.

The whole idea of being *for* something has gone out of style. Instead, we prefer to preach an angry "gospel" about whatever we have decided to stand *against*. We warm ourselves next to the fire of digital hashtags, ideologically slanted newsfeeds, political slogans, and religious doctrines, and then . . . ready, aim, fire! For the more popular voices among us, this can also become a great way to build a platform, gain followers and fans, and earn some cash.

Outrage sells.

For our generation, hate has been commodified. It has been turned into an asset.

THE POWER OF A GENTLE ANSWER

When *Saturday Night Live* comedian Pete Davidson crudely mocked Congressman-elect Dan Crenshaw because of his eye patch and flippantly remarked, "I know he lost his eye in the war or whatever," no one expected the former Navy SEAL and decorated war hero to respond to the insults in the way that he did. The mockery of Crenshaw's combat-inflicted disability, motivated by Davidson's disdain for his political views, resulted in such a strong public backlash that Davidson fell into depression and self-loathing. He wrote in an Instagram post, "I really don't want to be on this earth anymore. I'm doing my best to stay here for you but I actually don't know how much longer I can last. All I've ever tried to do was help people. Just remember I told you so."

Having lost his eye in combat in Afghanistan due to an explosion, some might have expected Crenshaw to say of Davidson, "Well, it serves him right." He could have added to the backlash or simply ignored the comedian. Instead, the veteran privately reached out to befriend, encourage, and speak life-giving words to Davidson. He told the comedian that everyone has a purpose in this world and that "God put you here for a reason. It's your job to find that purpose. And you should live that way."

Instead of firing back, Crenshaw built a bridge. Instead of

shaming and scolding, he spoke tenderly. Instead of seeking vindication through retaliation, he sought friendship through peacemaking. Instead of adding to the cycle of outrage, he soundly defeated outrage with a gesture of unconditional love.

Moved by compassion for the pain that Davidson had brought *upon himself* at Crenshaw's expense, the man trained in military strike and defense offered a gentle answer—so gentle, in fact, that it turned away the wrath of another man's political ire *and* the wrath of that same man's subsequent self-loathing. Then, on Veteran's Day weekend, the two came face-to-face on *Saturday Night Live* to make amends. Crenshaw offered warm remarks and high praise in reference to Davidson's own father, who was a New York City firefighter who died in the September 11, 2001, terrorist attacks when Davidson was seven years old. At the end of the segment, when he thought they were off camera, the embattled and humbled comedian leaned over to Crenshaw and whispered, "You are a good man."[3]

Such stories of kindness, forgiveness, and reconciliation can help us when we are faced with our own decisions. Do we take offense and strike back, or do we seek to extend kindness and offer a gentle answer? It applies when we are at odds with a family member, when we butt heads with a colleague, when our views are criticized online, when our children don't listen to or respect us, when someone rejects us because of our faith or our race or our social rank, or when we feel misunderstood by those of a different generation or economic situation or culture. In the midst of the tension, Jesus is there for us, just as he has been there for the likes of John Perkins, Dan Crenshaw, and the many others whose stories will be told in this book.

Those of us who identify as Christian have been given a

resource that enables us to respond to outrage and wrath in a healing, productive, and life-giving way. Because Jesus Christ has loved us at our worst, we can love others at their worst. Because Jesus Christ has forgiven us for all of our wrongs, we can forgive others who have wronged us. Because Jesus Christ offered a gentle answer instead of pouring out punishment and rejection for our offensive and sinful ways, we can offer gentle answers to those who behave offensively and sinfully toward us. But make no mistake: Jesus' gentle answer was bold and costly. His gentle answer included pouring out his lifeblood and dying on the cross. Our gentle answer will be costly as well. We must die to ourselves, to our self-righteousness, to our indignation, and to our outrage. For "whoever finds his life will lose it, and whoever loses his life for my sake will find it" (Matt. 10:39).

Jesus has been gentle toward us, so we have good reason to become gentle toward others, including those who treat us like enemies. "You have heard that it was said, 'You shall love your neighbor and hate your enemy.' But I say to you, Love your enemies and pray for those who persecute you, so that you may be sons of your Father who is in heaven" (Matt. 5:43–45). Because Jesus has covered all of our offenses, we can be among the least offensive and least offended people in the world. This is the way of the gentle answer.

HOW TO BENEFIT FROM THIS BOOK

A Gentle Answer is not a step-by-step how-to guide for becoming gentle. Instead, it attempts to answer the question, "What must happen in and around us so that we become *the kind of people* who offer a gentle answer?" We will seek answers together through various twists and turns, stories and anecdotes, and, most important, through encounters with the person and work of Jesus Christ. This book is as much about what must happen *to* us and *inside* us as it is about what must be done *by* us to engage faithfully in a world of us-against-them. It is as much about the forming and strengthening of our hearts toward a gentle, meek posture as it is about the behaviors and character attributes that naturally follow.

A Gentle Answer is organized into two parts. The first part examines how every Christian is a beneficiary of the gentleness of Jesus. This is the ultimate reason why every Christian's response to our us-against-them climate ought to be gentleness. As Jesus Christ befriends the sinner in us, reforms the Pharisee in us, and disarms the cynic in us, we find in him not only an example but the transformative resource that can inspire and empower gentleness in us. The second part examines the practical and obvious by-product of his gentleness toward us: namely, that we ourselves become gentle—as we grow thicker skin, handle anger well, receive criticism graciously, forgive all the way, and even bless our own betrayers. As you can see, the gentle answer has nothing to do with being weak. In fact, it requires the deepest, most courageous, and most heroic kind of faith—the kind that is possible only through the gentle and gentling power of Christ himself.

You'll also notice that each chapter ends with a few questions to consider. You can use these for personal reflection or (preferably) with a group of others who share your interest in embracing and advancing the way of gentleness. My sincere hope is that *A Gentle Answer*, which stands as a prequel and companion to my first book, *Jesus Outside the Lines: A Way Forward for Those Who*

Are Tired of Taking Sides, will serve as a roadmap for individual Christians, small groups, campus and other parachurch ministries, entire churches, and even networks and denominations, to defeat outrage and advance love. As in all Christian mission, these endeavors are best embarked upon *together* rather than in isolation.

The psalmist prayed to the Lord, "You have given me the shield of your salvation, and your right hand supported me, and your gentleness made me great" (Ps. 18:35). Whatever your story and however you choose to engage with this book, I pray the Lord will use its themes and stories to make you great in his gentleness.

PART I

THE GENTLENESS JESUS HAS FOR US

Come to me . . . and learn from me, for
I am gentle and lowly in heart . . . my
burden is light.

—Matthew 11:28–30

ONE

He Befriends the Sinner in Us

In the year 1874, William Gladstone was competing in the election for prime minister of the United Kingdom. Well known among his contemporaries for being a highly capable man by virtue of his sharp wit, expansive knowledge, and decorated track record, Gladstone was a formidable candidate for the role. Yet it was his opponent, Benjamin Disraeli, who seemed to have the endearing edge.

What made Disraeli more attractive to some was his widely known and celebrated ability to help people see their own value. While Gladstone had no problem helping people see how important *he* was as an accomplished man, Disraeli helped people see how important *they* were.

One evening, a woman named Jennie Jerome, famously known as the mother of Sir Winston Churchill, had an opportunity to converse with each of the candidates at a dinner party. When asked by a reporter about the experience and her impression of each of the candidates, she replied, "When I left the dining room after sitting next to Gladstone, I thought he was the cleverest man in England. But when I sat next to Disraeli, I left feeling that I was the cleverest woman."[1]

When we read through the four Gospels in the New Testament, it doesn't take long to see that Jesus bore similar features to both Gladstone and Disraeli. Like Gladstone, Jesus became widely known as a sharp, witty, intelligent, powerful man among his contemporaries. Though he had no formal education, crowds of people were astonished at the depth and profundity of his teaching. As it says in Luke's gospel regarding his teaching on the Sabbath, the people were "astonished at his teaching, for his word possessed authority" (Luke 4:32). Even today, we continue to marvel at his teachings such as the Sermon on the Mount, the Olivet Discourse, and his many parables. In addition to his teaching, Jesus also took transformative action that would bring life, health, and hope to the lives of others—healing the sick, comforting the downcast, defending the weak, and speaking truth to those in power.

However, like Disraeli, Jesus became widely known as one who helped others see their own value—not because he was a politician or candidate of any sort (he already was and is King over every square inch of the universe) and not because he was impressed with people's credentials or social stature. Instead, Jesus recognized that each person *does* have inherent value due to the image of God that is in him or her.

What is especially remarkable about Jesus' way of encouraging other people is not only *how* he affirmed their dignity but also *who* it was that he affirmed. Jesus gave a lot less attention to society's "important" people. Those who were accustomed to receiving VIP treatment, who sat at the head table at banquets, and who were esteemed in the temple and marketplace seemed not to be Jesus' primary focus. Instead, he turned his attention to those accustomed to being ignored, mistreated, discarded, and despised by the general public. If you were sick, poor, sexually damaged, or paralyzed by guilt and shame, for example, Jesus would move toward you and tell you what nobody else would: *you matter.*

Indeed, one of the most remarkable things about Jesus is his affection for and gentleness toward not the righteous, but sinners; not the healthy, but the sick; not those who have their act together, but those who are falling apart; not those who are clean, but those who are damaged and dirty. "This man welcomes sinners," the scribes and Pharisees charged, "and eats with them" (Luke 15:2 NIV). To the accusation of offering a gentle answer to sinners, Jesus was and is guilty as charged. When Jesus encountered people who recognized their own spiritual bankruptcy, he did not shame or belittle them—though he had every right to do so. Instead, he had a way of making them feel like the most significant, esteemed, and beloved people in the world.

We see this in Jesus' treatment of the man Zacchaeus, who will be our first case study. While most of us may not share Zacchaeus's shameful public reputation, or have the wealth and opulent lifestyle he accumulated chiefly through ill-gotten gain, sensitive souls will nevertheless see themselves in Zacchaeus. Specifically, they will see in themselves the same kind of sinner in need of the same kind of grace, mercy, and covering—the kind that only Jesus can provide. And hopefully, those same sensitive souls will come to experience the same gentle, gracious favor of Jesus hovering over them as it did over Zacchaeus.

GRACE FOR HUMANITY'S WORST

To the surprise of many, Jesus gave special, affirmational attention to the man Zacchaeus, who is identified in scripture as a chief tax collector (Luke 19:1–10). Because of his role as tax collector for the Roman treasury, Zacchaeus would have been hated by the members of his community. Tax collectors, and especially *chief* tax collectors, were known as what we might call white-collar thieves. These were men in power who made a habit of exploiting an unjust system—and specifically, the hardworking people living inside that system—for personal gain.

If you were a tax collector, government authorities would impose on you a quota for the amount of money you were to collect from citizens. Once your quota was satisfied, any further monies collected were yours to keep. This, of course, led most tax collectors to extort monies from citizens that were far above and beyond their actual tax burdens. To make matters worse, tax collectors lived opulent, self-indulgent lifestyles for all to see.

This ancient reality regarding tax collectors reminds me of a conversation I recently had with a woman who, like the citizens of first-century Rome, felt used and discarded by the powerful CEO of her company. According to this woman, the CEO made such extraordinary amounts of money that he was able to purchase several residential properties for himself in multiple major cities, all together totaling more than three hundred million dollars in value—a mere drop in the bucket compared to his accumulated net worth of more than ten billion dollars. The woman's issue with the CEO was not so much that he made a lot of money (in the Bible, God-fearing people like Abraham, Job, Solomon, and Joseph of Arimathea accumulate significant wealth and are not chided for it). Rather, her issue was that she found the work environment led by this man to be soul-sucking and dehumanizing. The number of hours that employees were expected to work were inhumane (sometimes more than eighty hours per week), their compensation and benefits were only enough to cover basic living needs, and their job security was so fragile that a person could lose her job at any given time, without warning. In her case, after requiring her to relocate from one city to another at her own expense, and although her work ethic and job performance in the company were excellent, she got laid off along with several others, with no reason given, just three months after her relocation. Having just signed a one-year apartment lease in her new and very expensive city, she was left unemployed and financially broke by what seemed to be a cold, self-serving decision made by a powerful and greedy man. Just weeks after she and several others were laid off, she read in the news that the CEO had, following the layoffs, purchased another home for himself worth more than two hundred million dollars.

Kind Gestures Toward the People We All Love to Hate

When a chief tax collector or a greedy CEO uses his power for selfish gain and in a way that leaves other people suffering, when he builds an opulent and seemingly carefree life for himself on the backs of hardworking, middle-class folk, it is understandable why many will look on him with contempt. This also helps us understand why tax collectors specifically were so despised in first-century Roman society. Who could feel anything but contempt for a powerful, self-serving crook? We can safely assume that, just like the greedy CEO among his former and discarded employees, Zacchaeus had no one in Jericho he could identify as a friend or a fan. When he walked through the crowds and climbed up into a sycamore tree to get a glimpse of Jesus, he did so all alone (Luke 19:1–4). His aloneness in the tree seems to communicate his costly reality—one that is not uncommon for powerful people who've built their empires by taking advantage of others—though he has become rich, he has also become isolated. Despised and rejected by men, his community esteemed him not. And so, he might have assumed that Jesus felt the same way about him. Maybe this is why, instead of approaching Jesus for a conversation, Zacchaeus climbed up into a tree to get a glimpse from a distance—not as a presumed or potential insider, but as an outsider looking in. As some might say, he knew his place.

Since first-century tax collectors were perhaps the most despised people in their communities, it is puzzling to observe how positively the Gospels seem to speak concerning them. In Luke's gospel, for example, tax collectors are mentioned six times—including the account of Zacchaeus—and in every instance the posture toward them is positive. In chapter three, tax collectors are baptized into the family of God. In chapter five, the tax collector Matthew is welcomed by Jesus into his circle of twelve disciples. (Matthew would later become the writer of the first of the four gospel accounts.) In chapter seven, tax collectors warmly and inquisitively receive Jesus teaching. In chapter fifteen, tax collectors and sinners gather around Jesus to hear him teach. In chapter eighteen, Jesus tells a parable of a smug, self-righteous religious man (who is sent home condemned and rejected) and a humble, penitent tax collector (who is sent home forgiven and accepted). Finally, in the Zacchaeus account in chapter nineteen, this man who is *chief* tax collector receives the gifts of friendship and salvation from Jesus.

The world looks at the likes of Zacchaeus and wants to judge, reprimand, and punish. Jesus, on the other hand, moves toward him, calls him by name, and offers to eat with him. Looking up at this lonely crook, Jesus says, "Zacchaeus, hurry and come down, for I must stay at your house today" (Luke 19:5).

What about the greedy CEO, then? Should we assume that Jesus would move toward him in friendship, also?

Or what about the man I met after a church service in Kansas City several years ago? This man, whom I had never met before, was a visitor to the church and requested a private conversation with me after the service was over. I had just finished preaching a sermon about the grace, love, and forgiveness of God, and how all of these gifts are available to any person who desires them. This man, whom I will call George to protect his confidentiality, asked me if I really meant it when I said the grace, love, and forgiveness of God could be for anyone. "Yes, of course I meant it," I replied.

George then told me something that he had never disclosed to anyone else. He confessed that he was a registered sex offender. Then he again asked, "Can this gospel, can Jesus Christ and the forgiveness and love and new beginning and embrace, can it really be *for me*? Or, now that you know this part of my story, would you like to change your answer?"

A part of me wanted to change my answer. Hearing George tell this part of his story made me feel protective of my young children, and it made me angry and afraid for them as well. If George had done this evil in the past, what would stop him from doing the same evil again? What's more, what kind of person do you have to be to *ever* do this sort of evil to another human being? How could anyone stoop so low as to use and abuse another human being like this? For a moment, I no longer wanted to tell George that the gospel of Jesus Christ could also be for him.

And then King David came to mind. King David saw Bathsheba, his next-door neighbor and wife of one of his most loyal friends and soldiers, Uriah the Hittite, bathing on her roof. He sent for her and, exploiting the power and authority of his office, *took* her for himself and had his way with her (2 Sam. 11:1–27). David, whom God's inspired Word would also refer to as "a man after his own heart" (1 Sam. 13:14), would later become author of half the Psalms. Jesus would call himself "the son of David" (see Matt. 1:1; 9:27; 12:23), and Luke, the writer of Acts, would also call him a man after God's own heart (Acts 13:22).

Gulp. It's true. If the grace, love, and forgiveness of God is available for the likes of David, it must also be available for the likes of George. So I responded to George, not with a revised answer, but with an even gentler version of the first: "No, I don't want to change my answer. I couldn't change it if I wanted to. Jesus wants to love you just as much as he wants to change you. He wants to help you with your demons just as he wants to help your victims with theirs. If your trust is in him, then Jesus is for you, George, just as he is for me. In the eyes of Jesus, you and I are both the same."[2]

The Scandal of a Gentle Answer

Extending kindness to the likes of Zacchaeus, King David, and George is precisely what made Jesus such a scandal among his contemporaries. The scandal around Jesus is a reality that distinguishes Christianity from every other world religion, as well as from all forms of human philosophy and politics: Jesus and Christianity do not discriminate between good people and bad people. Instead, Jesus and Christianity discriminate between humble people and proud people. "God opposes the proud but gives grace to the humble" (James 4:6).

Consider Jesus' ancestry—members of faith's "hall of fame" who were simultaneously and seasonally saint and sinner, virtuous and terrible, selfless and selfish, faithful and prodigal. Noah faithfully built the ark, and he also got drunk. Abraham believed the promises of God and walked courageously by faith, and he also handed his wife over to sex-hungry men twice in order to protect himself. Jacob became the father of the twelve tribes of Israel, and he also lied to secure a birthright that belonged to his brother. Solomon was the wisest man on earth, and he was also a womanizer. Rahab valiantly protected the Israelite spies, and she was also a sex worker.

In the Gospels we again see this "simultaneously saint and sinner" dynamic among the friends of Jesus. A despised Samaritan is made the hero of one of Jesus' most famous parables, as is a prodigal son who wishes his father dead and then squanders his inheritance on prostitutes and wild living. The religious folk disapproved of Jesus' questionable friendships and regularly reprimanded him for being a glutton, a drunk, and a friend of tax collectors and sinners (Matt. 11:19). Though Jesus was never actually guilty of being a glutton, a drunk, a greedy man, or a sinner, he was suspected of all of these and more because of the friendships he kept. He was, we might say, guilty by association.

Indeed, Jesus readily availed himself as friend and Savior to *outsiders and outlaws*,[3] to those regarded as losers and lowbrows and scumbags and pimps and whores and crooks. Maybe this is why the morally upright folk seemed to constantly take issue with Jesus. Maybe this is why they made a habit of criticizing him, discrediting him, belittling him, and becoming aggressive toward him. Maybe this is why they eventually killed him—because he welcomed sinners and ate with *them*.

But if you are Zacchaeus, instead of being repelled by Jesus, you are drawn irresistibly toward him. There is something about his kindness, something about his *gentleness* that makes Zacchaeus and others who, like him, have made a moral train wreck of their lives want to come out of the tree and have dinner with him. If you are Zacchaeus, you don't say in shock, "Jesus welcomes sinners and eats with *them*." Instead, you say with wonder and awe and gratitude, "Jesus welcomes sinners and eats with *us*."

This is the fundamental difference between human religion and Christianity. Whereas human religion puts the likes of Zacchaeus, the greedy CEO, and others like them into the category of "them" or "the bad people," Christianity says that we are all the same. All of us, without exception, are hopelessly stuck and isolated in sin and selfishness—unless and until Jesus looks up at us in the tree, calls us by name, and tells us to hurry up and come down to him because he is coming to our house today. Understanding this humbling reality, and letting it get massaged deeply into our hearts so that it reorients our posture, is an essential key to becoming instruments of God's grace, peace, and gentleness in a culture of outrage.

Christianity's Greatest Scandal Is Also Its Greatest Validation

Having been a Christian for thirty-four years and a minister for twenty-four, I have been told countless times by nonbelieving people that they would never consider becoming Christians because of all the Christians they know who are hypocrites. "So many Christians," the argument goes, "talk the talk, but don't walk the walk." As *Huffington Post* contributor Francis Maxwell has said, "Ahhh, Christianity in America. Or should I say, the single greatest cause of atheism today. . . . The type of people who acknowledge Jesus with their words, and deny him through their lifestyle." Citing broad ubiquitous evangelical support of immoral, predatory men who become political candidates and win elections with the widespread support of people who identify as Christian, Maxwell also writes, "It's okay to prey as long as you pray."[4]

The legitimacy of such concerns notwithstanding, what Francis Maxwell and many of my friends don't realize, and what I try to explain to them when given an opportunity, is that this very fact—that every single Christian *is* a hypocrite—is the whole basis for our Christian faith. As the Bible insists, Christ did not come into the world to affirm and accept the good people, but rather to rescue and receive the people who are not good. Being a religion of grace, Christianity doesn't have much to say to people, whether religious or secular, who build their lives and identities upon the idea of being good and virtuous. "Christ Jesus came into the world to save sinners," the apostle Paul wrote, "of whom I am the worst" (1 Tim. 1:15 NIV). "None is righteous, no, not one . . . no one does good, not even one" (Rom. 3:10–12). When asked, "Why do you eat and drink with tax collectors and sinners?" Jesus replied, "Those who are well have no need of a physician, but those who are sick. I have not come to call the righteous but sinners to repentance" (Luke 5:30–32).

So to say that Christians are hypocrites, that we fall short of the mark, that we don't keep the standard, is actually to affirm the chief tenet of our faith. It is to validate the very claim of Christ—that he came for sin-sick sinners who recognize that, apart from his rescue, they would hopelessly perish. While it is fair to call out Christians for hypocrisy, the hypocrisy in no way negates Christianity, but rather establishes it. In the same way that it would make zero sense to call Beethoven a substandard composer because a six-year-old plays a Beethoven piece sloppily and out of tune at a piano recital, it makes zero sense to call Jesus a substandard Savior because his followers imitate him poorly. I once heard Steve Brown, a pastor and radio personality from Florida, say that if we pastors were required to live without hypocrisy in every area about which we presumed to speak, we would have nothing left to preach. The same applies to every Christian, and every other human also. All honest people, whether religious or secular or otherwise, will be able to identify with the pronouncement that we are all, on some level, hypocrites. We all live inconsistently with the beliefs we profess.

One of my seminary professors once told our class about a conversation he had with the late Francis Schaeffer along these lines. Schaeffer, a well-known pastor, philosopher, and author, said that if we were all forced to carry a voice recorder around our necks that captured every conversation we've ever had and our conversations were made available for the rest of the world to hear, we would all go into hiding for the rest of our lives. Said differently, each and every one of us knows deep down that he or she is a hypocrite. "I do not understand what I do. For what I want to do I do not do, but what I hate I do" (Rom. 7:15 NIV). This is certainly true of me. Is it true of you?

As the life stories of Zacchaeus, King David, and others suggest, there is a significant and irreconcilable difference between "do-good religion" and Christianity. Whereas religion says, "If you do good, there will be a reward waiting for you at the finish line, and if you do bad, there will be punishment," Christianity says, "No one does good. But all is well nonetheless, because Jesus did not come for the righteous, but for sinners. He did not come for the good people who feel no need for him, but for humble people who know that without him, they are sunk. For those humble people, the reward is not given at the finish line, but rather at the starting line." Whereas religion presumes to work *for* the favor of God, life in Christ works *from* a favor that's already been given by God freely in Christ.

Perhaps this is why the poor-in-spirit tax collectors and sinners, much more so than the proud-in-spirit religious moralists, respond so swiftly and decisively when Jesus invites them to come down out of the tree and follow him. For he, and he alone, has the words of life (John 6:68). He, and he alone, can give a good name to bad men and women—and is therefore our ultimate source and power for the gentle answer.

A GOOD NAME GIVEN TO BAD MEN AND WOMEN

In the chapter of Luke's gospel prior to the Zacchaeus account, another more virtuous rich man encounters Jesus—a man we have come to know as "the rich young ruler." Unlike Zacchaeus, he is a religious man who has likely made his money through honest means. He has attended the temple faithfully, is a pillar of his religious and civic communities, and has, by his own account, kept the law of God since the days of his youth.

We are told Jesus looks at the rich man, loves him, and says to him that if he really wants to live, if he wants to be rich in the truest and most enduring sense of the word, he should sell all he has, give it to the poor, and then follow Jesus. Jesus does not offer this prescription to the young man because he has too much money, but because his money has too much of him. Recognizing that he has great wealth, the young ruler decides that Jesus' invitation is too much. So he turns around and he walks away sad.

Following this encounter, Jesus turns to his disciples and says, "How difficult it is for those who have wealth to enter the kingdom of God! . . . [I]t is easier for a camel to go through the eye of a needle than for a rich person to enter the kingdom of God." The disciples respond incredulously, "Then who can be saved?" Jesus comforts them with a gentle answer, saying, "What is impossible with man is possible with God" (Luke 18:24–30).

How sad that a virtuous, churchgoing kind of man—the rich young ruler—ends up missing out on the benefits of Christ and his eternal kingdom. How difficult it is for a rich person to enter the kingdom of God! And yet how wonderful that what is impossible with man is possible with God. So possible that another rich man—the lowly tax collector, Zacchaeus—receives salvation on the spot as he responds to Jesus' gentle, surprising invitation. "Zacchaeus! Hurry, come down, for I must stay at your house today." Once in Zacchaeus's house, Jesus declares, "Today salvation has come to this house, since he also is a son of Abraham. For the Son of Man came to seek and to save the lost" (Luke 19:9–10).

Did you catch that? The very man society deems as unredeemable, Jesus identifies as a son of Abraham, the father of all who are faithful. Because this is what Jesus does: He takes a bad name and turns it into a good name. He says to the outsider, "You belong," and to the outlaw, "Your sins will not be held against you," and to the shame and regret that drove the sinner up into the tree alone, "I'm coming to your house today. And there, in *your* house and on *your* turf, Zacchaeus, I'm going to show you a love and a hospitality like you've never dreamed. For your house and your turf, from this point forward, are going to be my house and my turf. I'm going to rearrange your furniture. I'm going to be your new decorator—both interior and exterior. I'm not coming to your house so you can serve me, but so I can serve you; not so you can feed me, but so I can feed you; not so you can take me in, but so I can take you in."

Belonging That Comes Before Believing

It is important to recognize that when Jesus tells Zacchaeus to come down from the tree, Zacchaeus is *still* a crook. He is, as Tolstoy has said, still walking along the road drunkenly, stumbling from side to side.[5]

This movement of Jesus toward Zacchaeus—*before* Zacchaeus does anything good or does anything for Jesus—is another feature of Christ that sets him apart from every other religious leader, philosopher, politician, or self-help guru. Jesus—like the Christian faith he came to establish—says to Zacchaeus and to every other person, "You belong even *before* you come to believe." We see this dynamic also in Jesus' interaction with the woman caught in the act of adultery. *Before* he says to her that she must leave her life of sin, he first assures her that as far as he is concerned, she is not condemned. "Neither do I condemn you," Jesus says, "go, and from now on sin no more" (John

8:11). If you reverse the order of these two sentences, if you say, "Leave your sin" *before* you will consider saying, "Neither do I condemn you," then you have ceased to speak the language of Christ, and you have ceased to reflect the heart of Christ. With Christ and with Christ-attuned Christians, belonging comes before believing.

This pattern is consistent through Scripture, in both Old and New Testaments. Before God gives the Ten Commandments to the people of Israel, he says to them, "I am the Lord your God, who brought you out of the land of Egypt, out of the house of slavery" (Ex. 20:2). In his letter to the church at Rome, the apostle Paul does not say that our repentance leads God to be kind to us. Instead, Paul writes that it is God's kindness that leads us to repent (Rom. 2:4). In his first letter to the church at Corinth, which is by far the most confrontational "leave your life of sin" letter in the New Testament, Paul first assures the Corinthian believers of their already established identity as God's beloved children, calling them "sanctified" and "saints" and recipients of God's grace and peace. He gives thanks for them, affirms his love for them, and reminds them that in Christ, God will sustain and keep them to the end, "guiltless in the day of our Lord Jesus Christ. God is faithful, by whom you were called into the fellowship of his Son, Jesus Christ our Lord" (1 Cor. 1:1–9). Then and only then does Paul begin to address the many sins and errors in their midst, including adultery, frivolous lawsuits, partisan rivalries, name dropping, neglecting the poor, sexual immorality, and the like. He does what the theologians call putting the indicatives (statements about *who* we are by virtue of *whose* we are in Christ) before the imperatives (statements about what we must become, and how we must now live, in light of who and whose we are).

The Double Scandal of Indicatives Before Imperatives

For many, this idea of putting indicatives before imperatives—offering love and acceptance instead of distance and punishment—comes across as scandalous. Responding to sin and selfishness with a gentle answer instead of retribution and shame seems offensive to those who are prone to separate the world into the good people and the bad people, as opposed to the proud people and the humble people. The offended will both think and say, "This idea of acceptance that comes before change in behavior is scandalous because it means that *they* are included—the tax collectors and the sinners!"

After the defeat of Hitler's Nazi regime in World War II, Holocaust survivor and Christian Corrie ten Boom returned to Germany to declare the forgiveness of Jesus Christ. One evening, after giving her message, she was approached by a man who identified himself as a former Nazi guard from the concentration camp at Ravensbruck, where she had been held and where her sister, Betsie, had died. When Corrie saw the man's face, she recognized him as one of the most cruel and vindictive guards from the camp. He reached out his hand and said to her, "A fine message, Fraulein! How good it is to know that, as you say, all our sins are at the bottom of the sea! You mentioned Ravensbruck in your talk. I was a guard there, but I would like to hear it from your lips as well. Fraulein, will you forgive me?" About this encounter, Corrie writes:

> I stood there—I whose sins had again and again been forgiven—and could not forgive. Betsie had died in that place. Could he erase her slow terrible death simply for the asking? It could have been many seconds that he stood there—hand held out—but to

> me it seemed hours as I wrestled with the most difficult thing I ever had to do . . . I had to do it—I knew that. The message that God forgives has a prior condition: that we forgive those who have injured us. . . . But forgiveness is not an emotion—I knew that too. Forgiveness is an act of the will, and the will can function regardless of the temperature of the heart. "Jesus, help me!" I prayed silently.

As she reached out her hand to the former guard, Corrie says that something incredible took place. She continues:

> The current started in my shoulder, raced down my arm, sprang into our joined hands. And then this healing warmth seemed to flood my whole being, bringing tears to my eyes. "I forgive you, brother!" I cried. "With all my heart!" . . . I had never known love so intensely, as I did then. But even then, I realized it was not my love . . . It was the power of the Holy Spirit.[6]

How remarkable that the gentleness of Jesus, who forgives our sins again and again, through that very act of forgiveness gentles *us*, thus empowering us—when our forgiveness is asked for—to grant it, even with all our hearts, to those who have injured us and the people we love most. A similar struggle and release occurred for the disciples in the early church when it was announced that Saul of Tarsus, who had acted as violently and cruelly toward Christians as the Ravensbruck guard, had been saved and welcomed by grace into the family of God (Acts 9:1–28). Likewise, the followers of Christ must have gone through a similar process when they discovered that Zacchaeus, who (along with other tax collectors) had stolen from them for years, was now one of them.

This gentle answer of welcome to sinners can be a double scandal—both to those who have been sinned against, like Corrie ten Boom, and to those who have committed the sins, like Zacchaeus. Astonished by the kindness and embrace extended to him by Jesus, Zacchaeus made an enthusiastic turn away from theft, greed, and the ways of self, and turned instead toward faith, generosity, and the ways of God. "Behold, Lord," the suddenly reformed crook says to Jesus, "the half of my goods I give to the poor. And if I have defrauded anyone of anything, I restore it fourfold" (Luke 19:8).

THE POWER OF GENTLE GRACE

Jesus invites us to come to him as we are—"Zacchaeus! Come down from that tree. I'm coming to your house today!"—but this must never be mistaken for an invitation to *stay* as we are. As was the case with Zacchaeus, so it is with us. When Jesus comes to our house, he doesn't do so merely to take our side.

He does so in order to take over.

His "I do not condemn you" always leads to the imperative, "Now leave your life of sin." He is not our consultant or adviser. He is not our personal assistant. He is our Lord. He has come to save us, and in saving us, to rearrange our furniture, to turn our house into his house, to become the interior and exterior designer of our lives, for the rest of our lives.

And what could be better than this? What could be better for Zacchaeus, the isolated crook, than to be made a friend of

Jesus and the people of Jesus, and a generous man to all? What could be better for Jacob, who lied to secure a birthright, than to be renamed "Israel" and made the father of the twelve tribes of God's people (Gen. 32:22–32)? What could be better for Peter, who struggled with both bravado and cowardice, than for Jesus to call his testimony that Jesus is truly the Messiah the rock upon which Jesus would build his church (Matt. 16:18)? What could be better for David, the murderer and adulterer and sexual predator, than to be commissioned as writer of half the Psalms, identified as the man after God's own heart as well as the esteemed ancestor of the Son of God, who would delight in calling himself the son of David (Matt. 1:6)? What could be better for Rahab, the Canaanite prostitute, than to be included in Jesus' genealogy and inducted into faith's hall of fame—not as a scandalous or beaten-down sex worker but as a cherished, purified princess (Heb. 11:31)?

It turns out that the power of Jesus' gentle grace, which includes receiving a new name and new identity and new way of life, turns away not only wrath but also so much more. It turns away foolishness, selfishness, greed, immorality, abuse, violence, gossip, slander, deceit, and all things from which we desperately need rescue. The gentle answer of Jesus gives us the power not merely to turn over a new leaf, but to have a new life.[7] "Truly, truly, I say to you, I am the door of the sheep," Jesus said. "All who came before me are thieves and robbers, but the sheep did not listen to them. I am the door. If anyone enters by me, he will be saved and will go in and out and find pasture. The thief comes only to steal and kill and destroy. I came that they may have life and have it abundantly" (John 10:7–10).

As Zacchaeus can attest, even thieves can get in on the ways of Jesus. Will we welcome Jesus into our house today, as well?

QUESTIONS FOR REFLECTION AND DISCUSSION

1. Name one thing from this chapter that troubled you, inspired you, or both. Why were you impacted in this way?
2. In today's society, who are the Zacchaeus types that everybody seems to despise? What qualities would turn another person into a Zacchaeus type in *your* eyes? How do you feel, and what do you think, about the idea of Jesus reaching out to that person with the same degree of love and acceptance that he gives to you? Does the thought warm you, offend you, or both? Why do you answer in the way that you do?
3. In what ways do you relate to Zacchaeus as the man in the tree? In what ways do you relate to him as the man who became a friend of Jesus? As the man whose life was radically transformed? Why do you think that God put the story of Zacchaeus in the Bible—as opposed to the story of a morally upright citizen?
4. Based on this chapter, identify one way that the Lord might be nudging you toward growth or change. What steps should you take to pursue the change?

TWO

He Reforms the Pharisee in Us

Some readers may be tempted to skip this chapter because of its title. "Why would I need to read about the Pharisee in me when everything in me bristles at the Pharisees I read about in the Bible? I can't stand their holier-than-thou, smug, hyper-critical, stuffy ways. How, then, does this chapter relate to me?"

If you have a similar internal monologue, you may want to consider whether it is a sign that you *do*, in fact, possess an inner Pharisee. Whenever a feeling rises in us that resembles the Pharisee's prayer, "Thank you, my God, that I am not like other men!" (see Luke 18:9–14), the most important thing we can do is pause, take inventory of our hearts, and run to Jesus for clarity and also for mercy—even, and perhaps especially, when the *other people* we are repudiating and condemning are the Pharisees themselves. In our certainty that we are not like them, we ironically show ourselves to be among them.

One very subtle way that our inner Pharisee shows up is when we disassociate ourselves from historically and biblically

Christian endeavors—ones like attending a local church, identifying publicly as followers of Christ, or sharing our faith with others—because of how *other people* have given a bad name to such endeavors. "So many so-called Christians have given such a bad, embarrassing name to Christianity," we tell ourselves, "and I am so upset about it! I am not going to associate with other Christians anymore, lest I be lumped in as one of them." We can think this even though Jesus was always willing to associate with his own woefully imperfect followers—the abrasive and cowardly Peter and the formerly blasphemous, persecuting, and violent Paul being two cases in point. Yet the Pharisee in us is unwilling to do the same. In fact, it bristles at the idea.

"I am better than this," the inner Pharisee tells us.

"I am above this."

Not so fast.

THE DEATH OF EVANGELISM?

Have you ever been so positively impacted by something that you felt you *must* tell others about it? In the Bible, this kind of enthusiastic sharing is called *evangelism,* the proclamation of good news with the goal of persuading others to receive it and orient their lives around it.

There are many reasons for evangelism, and not all of them are religious in nature. If we have a delicious meal at the newest restaurant in town, we will spread the word to others that they *must* dine there too. If a therapist helps us heal from anxiety and depression or guides a difficult family situation back toward health, we will warmly urge other strugglers to visit the same therapist. If our favorite line of clothing or pair of shoes goes on sale, we will want to share the news. If a particular diet and exercise program, a piece of music, a book, a poem, a painting, a nonprofit organization, or a church community contributes to our joy and flourishing, we will try to draw others into the experience as well. When something brings meaning to our lives, our enjoyment of the thing is made most complete when we share it with others.

C. S. Lewis summarized this evangelistic impulse when he wrote, "I think we delight to praise what we enjoy because the praise not merely expresses but completes the enjoyment; it is its appointed consummation . . . It is frustrating to have discovered a new author and not be able to tell anyone how good he is . . . to hear a good joke and find no one to share it with."[1]

Based on our instinct to share with others what brings us meaning, one wonders if the chief reason—or at least one of the chief reasons—Jesus gave us the Great Commission was to make our own joy complete. Yet, curiously, there is currently a glaring exception to the evangelistic impulse that we will want to tell others about the things that bring our lives the most meaning. This exception is that, today, American Christians are often reluctant to express their enthusiasm about Jesus Christ with other people. Unlike Peter and Paul and the other disciples who preached boldly, confidently, and joyfully from town to town (Acts 14:21), unlike the Samaritan woman who couldn't wait to tell everyone she knew about her encounter with Jesus (John 4:1–42), and unlike so many believers around the world who will even risk their lives to get the saving message of Christ out to their neighbors, many American Christians prefer to keep their good news about Jesus hidden. In fact, some are not only reluctant but also opposed to the practice of trying to encourage other people to trust and follow Jesus.

SURVEY SAYS . . .

According to a 2019 report from the Barna Group, an increasing number of Christians have entirely backed away from sharing their faith. Specifically, almost half of millennials (those born between the early 1980s and early 2000s) who identify as followers of Jesus say that evangelism isn't just uncomfortable, but that it is actually *wrong.* According to the report, 97 percent of Christians across four generations—millennials, Generation X, baby boomers, and elders—agree with the statement, "The best thing that could ever happen to someone is for them to come to know Jesus." At the same time, 47 percent of millennials, plus smaller but still significant percentages from the other three generations, agree that "It is wrong to share one's personal beliefs with someone of a different faith in hopes that they will one day share the same faith."[2]

Yes, you read correctly. On the one hand, American Christians believe almost unanimously that the very *best* thing that can happen to a person is to have a saving relationship with Jesus Christ. On the other hand, many from the same group also believe that the very *worst* thing a Christian can do is persuade people to come into a relationship with Jesus Christ.

What in the world is going on here?

This strange dissonance can be attributed to the fact that today's Christians are viewed differently by their neighbors than first-century Christians were by theirs. In the book of Acts, we are told that early Christians lived and loved so remarkably among their neighbors that they were "having favor with all the people" (Acts 2:47). This does not mean they were without enemies. In fact, the powerful religious establishment was so opposed to the Christian movement that they urged Pontius Pilate, the governor of Judea, to crucify Jesus without legitimate cause (Luke 23:21). Similarly, the early Christians' belief that *Jesus* was Lord as opposed to the Roman Caesar got many of them imprisoned and/or executed. Jesus' instruction to his disciples in this environment was not to avoid, hate, or retaliate against their enemies. Instead, they were to love their enemies (Matt. 5:43–48).

Even though the persecution of Christians was common, the average Roman citizen held Christians in high esteem because of how life-giving they were as neighbors. If you were poor, sick, disabled, a widow, an abused woman, or an at-risk child, you knew that the Jesus followers who gathered as a local church were the best people to go to for love, acceptance, nonjudgmentalism, and care for your physical, emotional, financial, and spiritual needs. Though Rome had all the resources and power, the early Christians ran circles around the government in the way that they cared for their Roman neighbors. Given this generous posture among Christians in the places where they lived, worked, and played, it's no wonder they were having favor with all.

Over the years, and especially in Western culture, this dynamic between Christians and their neighbors has shifted. Rather than being esteemed as the best kinds of friends to the world around us, we are often regarded as the worst kinds of enemies. Rather than having favor with all, we have disfavor with many. Three key factors contribute to this shift.

Reasons for the Shift

First, many who currently oppose Christianity do so because of what they regard as hypocrisy among Christians. Some will cite atrocities done in the name of Christ through history: slavery, racism, the subjugation of women, genocide, and other evils. Others will cite the many public scandals, including sexual abuse and pedophilia in both Protestant and Catholic churches, as well as things like abuse of power, bullying, harsh or neglectful parenting, marital infidelity, pornography habits, and/or misuse of funds by well-known pastors and priests. These days, it seems, a scandal or two hits the news cycle every month. Still others will cite their own personal negative experiences with Christians. Terms such as *narrow-minded, judgmental, holier-than-thou, uncompassionate,* and *blindly partisan* are used to describe Christians by their non-Christian neighbors.

A second reason for this cultural shift is that many in today's society find the conflation of Christianity and partisan politics to be offensive. Generally speaking, older believers—evangelicals in particular—treat right-leaning political causes, including ones that seem incongruent with principles of biblical compassion, as being one and the same with their idea of faithful Christianity. One woman who grew up in the church wrote in the *Huffington Post* of her desire to disassociate from Christianity for this very reason, "I don't want to call myself a Christian anymore . . . For years, I wore that label comfortably and confidently, as it has been the core of my identity since my earliest memories. But now, that label makes me uncomfortable, and even disgusted, and I want the rest of my life to be defined by something different."[3]

The woman goes on to tell of her family upbringing. They attended church every Sunday, prayed before dinner, and read the Bible at bedtime. She went to church camps, youth retreats, Christian concerts, attended a Christian school, and pledged a Christian sorority. But lately, she has become "horrified and embarrassed" about American Christianity in particular, which she believes promotes nationalism, political agendas that damage and overlook those who are poor and sick and vulnerable, and political leaders whose personal lives are filled with dishonesty, greed, predation, and misogyny. She concludes, "I really don't know where I go from here. I'm frustrated, angry, and lonely. I've lost friends, and the foundation of my entire life has been cracked, probably irreparably . . . I still want to be a Christian, but need a new definition of what that truly means."[4]

As this woman's story attests, many who are drawn to follow Jesus are also distancing themselves from movements and traditions that seem more politically partisan and less spiritual in nature. When "love your neighbor" takes a back seat to American partisanship, when the protection and advancement of our own rights and privileges take precedence over the needs of the least of these, spiritually and socially sensitive people can find it difficult to get on board with versions of Christianity that look, smell, and talk more like Uncle Sam than like Jesus Christ.

A third and related reason for the shift from favor to disfavor toward Christians is that many people today perceive that Christians lack humility, approachability, and empathy. Ask the average skeptic, agnostic, or atheist what they think Christianity stands for, and she will likely respond by saying that Christianity is about being right, acting superior *in* your rightness, and injuring people *with* your rightness. In the *Huffington Post* essay previously mentioned, the woman also describes a discriminatory posture she has observed in some Christian churches, where bulletins boast the taglines "Come as You Are," yet simultaneously also communicate, "But wait, not if you're gay"[5]—or for that matter not if you dress, vote, or worship incorrectly, or if you don't share our race or our economic situation or our cultural values, as the case may be.

Whenever I hear Christians spoken of in this way—as being more exclusive than inclusive, more judgmental than kind, more off-putting than inviting, more standoffish than welcoming—I am reminded of a scene from the movie *Saved!* In this scene, a high school girl named Hilary Faye (played by Mandy Moore)—known for being the school's most religiously devout student, the principal's favorite, and the self-appointed lead singer for a teen band called the Christian Jewels—scolds another girl, Mary, who is struggling with doubting her faith, losing her virginity, and an unplanned pregnancy:

> **Hilary Faye:** Mary, turn away from Satan. Jesus, he loves you.
>
> **Mary:** You don't know the first thing about love.
>
> **Hilary Faye:** [throws a Bible at Mary] I am *filled* with Christ's love! You are just jealous of my success in the Lord.
>
> **Mary:** [holds up the Bible] This is not a weapon! You idiot.[6]

Counterfeits of Christianity have earned for Christianity *itself* a black eye in today's cultural climate. Perceived by many as hypocritical, excessively partisan, and fixated on attacking the specks in others' eyes while ignoring the planks in our own, it's no wonder that Christians, especially younger ones, have become disenchanted with the idea of sharing their faith. For who among them would want to publicly associate with a movement that seems characterized more by judgment and scorn than by grace and love? This is at least in part why even sincere believers in Jesus are starting to disassociate themselves from labels such as *evangelical* and *Christian* that have given a bad name both to Jesus and to them, but without their participation or consent. They are reluctant to enter the fray for fear of being found guilty by association and to be judged by the world in the same way that many in the world have felt judged by Christians.

Jesus: The Refreshing Alternative to Those Who Represent Him Poorly

Contrary to those who represent him in hypocritical and counterfeit ways, Jesus was always perfect, never erring even once in his thoughts, words, or actions. His teaching and content were perfect, and so were his tone and posture. Unlike his scribe and Pharisee contemporaries, Jesus did *not* belittle or behave condescendingly toward people, especially those who had become accustomed to being treated as outsiders. Rather than shaming and scolding sinners, Jesus welcomed sinners and ate with them—with such open arms that it got him accused of being a glutton and a drunk (Matt. 11:19). He was accused of such things not because he actually was a glutton or a drunk, but rather because of the people with whom he decided to become a friend.

Little children, prostitutes, tax collectors, sinners, people who lacked education, the poor and the sick and the unemployed, lepers, crooks, addicts, people with disabilities and special needs, the elderly, and misfits all felt worse and more burdened after encountering the scribes and Pharisees . . . but they felt better and less burdened after encountering Jesus. For Jesus not only said the words, "Come to me, all you who are weary and burdened, and I will give you rest" (Matt. 11:28 NIV). He also lived and embodied them.

When Jesus spent time with humble and/or hurting people, they would feel seen, dignified, esteemed, loved, and hopeful. Jesus promised that his yoke would be easy and his burden would be light; that his presence would be a haven of rest for those who were tired of religion and tired of themselves; that he would be a physician for the sick, an encourager for the shame-ridden, and even a lover of his enemies. This caused all sorts of downtrodden and morally fatigued people to gain new hope, find new rest, and taste new freedoms. Jesus' effect on people was to take their burdens off them, as opposed to putting more burdens on them. Jesus, we might say, was not only the best kind of friend to such souls. He was also the best kind of enemy. Jesus, the One who insisted that we must love even our enemies, personally showed us the way.

To remind our Nashville congregation of this aspect of Jesus' nature—that he is a lover of his enemies—we often guide them in our Sunday services through the following liturgical confession leading up to the Lord's Supper:

Leader: What right do we have to dine at the Table of Jesus?

Family: We have every right to dine at his Table.

Leader: What gives us this right?

Family: We have this right because Jesus came not for the strong, but for the weak; not for the righteous, but for sinners; not for the

> self-sufficient, but for those who know they need rescue. To all who are weary and need rest; to all who mourn and long for comfort; to all who feel worthless and wonder if God even cares; to all who are weak and frail and desire strength; to all who sin and need a Savior—Jesus welcomes into his circle, adopts into his family, and reserves a place at his Table. For he is the mighty friend of sinners, the ally of his enemies, the defender of the indefensible, and the justifier of those who have no excuses left.[7]

Indeed, Jesus came to turn his enemies into friends, his friends into family, and his family into joyful participants in his mission. It is Jesus' own gentle spirit that turns his people into gentle evangelists of his name. He is the God of those who know themselves to be weak, sinful, in need of rescue, guilty of indefensible things, and void of legitimate excuses. "God shows his love for us," the apostle Paul writes, "in that while we were still sinners, Christ died for us" (Rom. 5:8). While we were running away from him and not toward him, while we were hostile and opposed to him and not favorable toward him, while we were his enemies and not his friends, while we were still sinners . . . *that* is the moral setting in which Christ showed to us the full extent of his love. *That* is when the gentle yet powerful love of Christ became most visible and real to us. By our own merit we are by no means his choice people, but by faith we are his chosen people—known and loved, exposed and not rejected, offensive yet embraced, adopted by grace through faith and bringing no moral capital of our own to the table. It is his gentleness alone—complete with his kindhearted care, his unmerited love, the turning away of his wrath from us—that should have, over time, the effect of turning our wrath away from him and from our neighbors.

THE PRIDE OF THE SCRIBES AND PHARISEES

Why is the world's experience of Christians so different than Christians' experience of Christ? Why aren't God's people reflecting his gentleness, truth, and love? This problem is not new. Jesus addressed this disconnect and often focused on how the misguided Pharisees and other smug religious leaders not only misrepresented God, but also pushed people away instead of gently leading them toward the truth and freedom of the kingdom of God. When Jesus spoke of the scribes and Pharisees, he said, "[They] sit in Moses' seat" (Matt. 23:2 NIV). The term *Moses' seat* was a Jewish idiom meaning that they were teachers of scripture: specifically, of the five books of Moses—Genesis, Exodus, Leviticus, Numbers, and Deuteronomy. In those days, these five books were the only Bible they had in their possession. The scribes, like professional theologians, interpreted scripture for the community. Their job was to explain to people the *meaning* of each section of the five books of Moses. The Pharisees, who worked alongside the scribes, were like professional ministers who were responsible for shepherding the people as they put the scriptures into practice in daily life. While the scribes were responsible for interpreting scripture, the Pharisees were responsible for building a code of *ethics* based upon those interpretations.

Somewhere along the way, both the scribes and the Pharisees

lost their way. Rather than letting themselves be handled *by* the Word of God, they presumed themselves to be handlers *of* the Word of God. Rather than standing beneath the Word of God, they started using the Word of God as a tool with which to exalt themselves over other people . . . and even over God himself. Jesus' parable of a Pharisee and tax collector comes to mind, in which the Pharisee congratulates himself for his stellar piety, mentioning himself eight times and God only once. The Pharisee then turns his focus toward others, viewing them with contempt as he prays, "God, I thank you that I am not like other men" (Luke 18:9–14).

In a confrontational encounter, Jesus stated publicly that the scribes and Pharisees did *all* of their deeds not as a service to God, but rather as a means by which to be recognized and applauded by people. "The scribes and the Pharisees sit on Moses' seat," Jesus said, "so do and observe whatever they tell you, but not the works they do. For they preach, but do not practice. They tie up heavy burdens, hard to bear, and lay them on people's shoulders . . . They do all their deeds to be seen by others" (Matt. 23:2–8). In other words, they were using God to control people and to manipulate others into thinking that *they* were praiseworthy.

Jesus made a habit of exposing and confronting how the scribes and Pharisees flaunted their faith, sought the best seats at banquets and in the synagogue, and used religion as a means to secure for themselves recognition and titles. Jesus' Sermon on the Mount gets specific and exposes the motivations beneath their financial generosity, their public prayers, and their pious behaviors (see Matt. 5–7). These self-serving religious leaders wanted VIP treatment more than they wanted God. As Eugene Peterson aptly paraphrases in *The Message*, with the scribes and Pharisees "It's all spit-and-polish veneer," like a perpetual fashion show

(Matt. 23:3 MSG). From their perspective, religion was their costume, people were their audience, and God was their stagehand and supporting actor. As long as you (or God) supported them in this self-exalting endeavor, they would refrain from judging and punishing you. But if you dared to cross them, challenge them, or fall out of accord with their list of nonnegotiable and man-made traditions, they would turn against you.

Religious Pride as a Gentleness Killer

We must not shake our heads and sneer at the foolish pride of the Pharisees. The deception and darkness of self-glory and self-sufficiency began in the garden when Adam and Eve doubted God and sought their own advancement, and it continues to seek to reign in every single human soul. How can we detect when this self-serving spirit creeps into our own hearts? For me, it tends to show up in the form of ambition. For example, if I find myself starting to enjoy the sound of my own name more than the sound of Jesus' name, I know that I have gotten off-center. Or if I find myself becoming more zealous for my reputation than I am for Jesus' reputation in the world, I am likewise headed in a wrong and damaging direction. How about you?

In whatever way it surfaces, the self-exalting, self-salvation project of the scribes and Pharisees—the project that emphasizes keeping rules over loving God and people, working hard to impress over resting in grace, and performing duties over celebrating the finished work of Jesus Christ—becomes a poor counterfeit for biblical Christianity. When we choose the substitute, we will eventually start hating ourselves for failing at the project, hating others for not supporting our agenda, and/or hating God for not rewarding us with the life we think we deserve.

One tragic (but fictional) portrayal of turning hostile toward God was portrayed in the Oscar-winning film *Amadeus*, based on the play by Peter Shaffer. At one point in the film, the composer Antonio Salieri attempts to bargain with God. If God will give him fame, Salieri prays, he will return the favor by living a chaste, righteous life. Furthermore, he will give glory to God alone for his music. As the film progresses, however, it becomes apparent that God has no interest in Salieri's proposal. For the only kind of worship and service God accepts is the kind in which we worship and serve him for his own sake, and not as a means to some other desired end.

When a rival composer, Wolfgang Amadeus Mozart, enters the scene, he does so as a vile, drunk, womanizing, obscene specimen of a man who is also—much to Salieri's chagrin—a world-class composer. Before long, Mozart upstages Salieri, who spirals into deep resentment. Though he is hardworking, responsible, and devoted to his craft, Salieri becomes a lesser-than, mediocre, and even laughable artist in the eyes of his peers and society in comparison to Mozart's genius. In one scene, Mozart mockingly bangs out a Salieri piece on a piano at a dinner party, humiliating Salieri in front of all the guests. Wanting to be famous, Salieri is made—at least in his own eyes—a *persona non grata*.

Instead of accepting God's will for him and for Mozart, Salieri erupts in rage and turns against God. He prays a second prayer, this time with less of a plea and more of an accusation, saying, "From now on we are enemies, you and I. Because you choose for your instrument a boastful, lustful, smutty, infantile boy and give me only the ability to recognize the incarnation. Because you are unjust, unfair, unkind, I will block you, I swear it. I will hinder and harm your creature on Earth as far as I am able. I will ruin your incarnation."[8]

As one might imagine, the only person Salieri ended up ruining was himself. In becoming an enemy to God, he became his own worst enemy. And it all began with the seeds of the self-exalting scribe and Pharisee spirit which—when nurtured and watered by human entitlement and self-pity and resentment instead of the fruit of gratitude, love, and gentleness—turned into a sprout, then into a tree, then into a forest, then into an outright forest fire of abrasiveness and aggression and resentment of God and neighbor.

Pride, as the proverb says, goes before a fall (Prov. 16:18). Not only this, pride steals from us the joy of surrender to a loving, wise God who writes our stories much better than we ever could. This joy and rest are replaced with soul-sucking, community-killing, envy-feeding, hate-filled, rivalrous resentment—not only toward people but toward God himself. In such a tumultuous moral and emotional climate, a gentle posture becomes the furthest thing from our reality. By our own undoing, we will become aliens to the kingdom, purposes, mission, and rest-giving embrace of God. Tragically, we will lose tender affection for God as well as gentleness toward our neighbor.

ANOTHER KIND OF PHARISEE

At this point, those who pride themselves as being more progressive and tolerant and less strident than the scribes and Pharisees might be thinking, "Yes, this—the spirit of the scribe and Pharisee—*this* is exactly why I've grown so weary of and impatient toward Christians. As far as I am concerned, their loveless and intolerant pride makes them unlovable and intolerable! I have great respect for Jesus Christ, but I don't want in any way to be associated with those who identify as his followers. By their smug attitudes and behaviors, these people give Jesus and Christianity and religion a bad name. It is because of *them* that people like me don't want to be associated with words like *evangelical* or *Christian* anymore. I want to be spiritual, but not religious. People like me want to love people rather than lecture them, to accept people rather than try to change their minds, to embrace diversity rather than proselytize, to lovingly affirm people for who they are rather than offensively suggest they are wrong, to let them live their truth rather than impose my truth upon them."

These sorts of concerns toward loveless expressions of religious pride are understandable. When faith becomes sour and starts to look and feel like all law and no love, all truth and no grace, all judgment and no embrace, all exclusion and no welcome, it's clear we have drifted from the heart and ways of Jesus Christ. This becomes a Christianity void of Christ, which, of course, is not Christianity at all, but a farce.

At the same time, such strong negative feelings and sneering toward Pharisees *themselves* (as opposed to an acknowledgment of the strident, miserable spirit in which they have become stuck) can also be a smokescreen for a different agenda. Some condemn Pharisees in order to keep their distance from biblical truths and commands that make them uncomfortable. But even Jesus said of the Pharisees, "Observe whatever they tell you" (insofar as what they tell you is congruent with scripture), "but not the works they do" (Matt. 23:3). In other words, just as we shouldn't shoot the messenger because of a message we find difficult, neither should we shoot the message because of *messengers* we find difficult. Don't throw the baby out with the bath water. We must be careful not to reject something true and good, the teachings of Scripture, in an effort to get rid of something dirty that needs to be removed—the self-serving, erroneous ways of the Pharisees. If we are harboring an agenda to protect ourselves from having to deal with certain parts of God's Word so as to free ourselves to think, believe, and live however we choose, we are no different than the scribes and the Pharisees. We, like them, are being selective with a body of truth (Scripture) that is intended to be received comprehensively and not merely in part. Detecting our own strong, self-righteous reaction to the Pharisee is a good reason to examine our own motives. Is our real reason for being upset with the Pharisee because we believe deep down that nobody, including God, has a right to tell us how are we supposed to think, believe, or live?

If we are not careful, we risk swinging the pendulum from loveless or conservative pride to lawless or liberal pride. Especially in the modern West, there are forms of liberalism that can become a breeding ground for entitlement, resentment, separation, tribalizing, echo chambers, and scorn. Under the false pretense of tolerance, liberal pride can lead its adherents into forms of exclusiveness and name-calling and injurious behavior that are quite Phariseelike. Some of the world's most intolerant people are those who refuse to tolerate anyone they deem to be less "tolerant" than they are.

In his popular *New York Times* essay entitled, "A Confession of Liberal Intolerance," journalist Nicholas Kristof, himself a self-avowed liberal, confesses this inconsistency among those in his own ideological and political tribe. He candidly and humbly wrote, "We progressives believe in diversity, and we want women, blacks, Latinos, gays and Muslims at the table—er, so long as they aren't conservatives. Universities are the bedrock of progressive values, but the one kind of diversity that universities disregard is ideological and religious. We're fine with people who don't look like us, as long as they think like us . . . [This illuminates] liberal arrogance—the implication that conservatives don't have anything significant to add to the discussion. My [liberal followers] have incredible compassion for war victims in South Sudan, for kids who have been trafficked, even for abused chickens, but no obvious empathy for conservative scholars facing discrimination . . . So it's easier to find a Marxist in some [academic] disciplines than a Republican . . . The discrimination becomes worse if [someone is] an evangelical Christian."[9]

The sociologist George Yancy, who is both black and an evangelical, agreed, observing, "Outside of academia I faced more problems as a black. But inside academia I face more problems as a Christian, and it is not even close."[10]

Indeed, on all sides, there is plenty of hypocritical smugness to go around.

Whether conservative or progressive, whether religious or nonreligious, we must be careful, in our passionate zeal against the spirit of the unloving Pharisee, that we do not become unloving Pharisees ourselves—a hate group who is harsh, manipulative, and condemning with anyone who disagrees with us. This truth applies not only along ideological and doctrinal lines but also along economic and cultural and moral ones.

WILLIAM

One Sunday during a worship service at church, a man I had never met strolled into the sanctuary, gingerly sipping a cup of coffee.

This man stood out in the crowd because he wore filthy, torn-up jeans and a cut-off T-shirt. His arms were tatted up with ink and covered with scars and needle streaks. If you stood within ten feet of him, you could smell the reek of cigarette smoke and body odor. His name, I would find out later that morning, was William.

As the congregation sang a worship song together, a man in the church wearing fine clothing, whom I will refer to as Church Guy, tapped me on the shoulder and pointed over at William. "Do you see that man over there?" he asked. "Yes, I sure do," I replied. Church Guy continued, "He has a lot of nerve entering the house of God dressed in filthy, ratty clothes like that. And who told him it was okay to bring coffee into the sanctuary? You can smell the nicotine from a mile away. *He is a distraction to my worship.* Pastor, do you want me to talk to him about these things? Do you want me to go over there and tell him how people are supposed to behave in the house of God?" My heart sank over his words. "No thanks," I replied. "I've got this."

As Church Guy returned to his seat, I was reminded of a passage in James, where the apostle and half-brother of Jesus wrote about situations like this. "If a man wearing . . . fine clothing comes into your assembly, and a poor man in shabby clothing also comes in, and if . . . you say to the poor man, 'You stand over there . . .' have you not then made distinctions among yourselves and become judges with evil thoughts? Listen, my beloved brothers, has not God chosen those who are poor in the world to be rich in faith and heirs of the kingdom . . . ? But you have dishonored the poor man" (James 2:2–6).

So instead of sending Church Guy over to talk to William, I asked Mark, himself a recovering addict, to be sure that he greeted and befriended William after the service. Mark discovered that

William was one month sober from a drug addiction and had come to our church because the people in his recovery program told him that being part of a religious community would increase his chances of staying sober.

Beginning with this initial, warm welcome from Mark, William became a valued member of our church community. He was not ignored or treated as lesser than, but was celebrated and treated as important because, according to James, that's what you should do when someone has the courage to enter in with shabby and stinky clothing, a hard-fought story of survival, and a thirst for deliverance from the many demons that have haunted him.

As far as I know, Church Guy never introduced himself to William. Instead, he continued to keep his distance, clinging to a hollow form of religion without grace, rules without relationship, and law without any evidence of love.

RECEIVING AND EXTENDING A GENTLE INVITATION

That day when Church Guy said those things about William, I drove home infuriated. In the car I began to express out loud my frustration about Church Guy's crushing blindness and judgmental spirit. "Who does he think he is? Who is he to criticize and condemn this clearly hurting and *courageous* visitor? I'm not sure what Church Guy calls an addict who has just traded in his heroin addiction for a nicotine addiction. But as I see it, you ought to call it progress. Doesn't he know it's not the healthy who need a doctor, but the sick? Jesus did not come to call the righteous, but sinners!" (Mark 2:17).

Clearly, Church Guy was not the only guy dishing out law without love that day. During my car ride home I also gave God a bit of advice, perhaps in the same way that Salieri offered a bargain to God in the film *Amadeus*. I told God that the biggest problem with church these days, and the thing that makes it hardest to be a pastor, is Church Guys. "Why on earth," I prayed, "would you allow your church—*our* church, *my* church—to be infected with smug, holier-than-thou, plank-in-the-eye, shaming, scolding Church Guys? Who on earth says that a broken, cluttered-up man in our midst is a distraction to our worship? Shouldn't the presence of such a man be an *enhancement* of our worship and just one more reason to fall on our faces in awe of your grace, mercy, kindness, gentleness, and love? Ugh! As I see it, Lord, the biggest problem with church is all the Pharisee Church Guys!"

I do believe that sometimes God can speak to people audibly, although thus far I have not been one of them. But if God ever did speak to me directly and unmistakably, it was to my soul in that very moment, after my rant about Church Guys and Pharisees. To my soul, the Holy Spirit whispered, "Scott, my child, to indulge this grudge—as you have against the man you call Church Guy—you have yourself *become* the very worst things you loathe in Church Guy. Your ranting against the unloving Pharisee in your midst confirms that you, Scott, are an unloving Pharisee toward those you deem unloving Pharisees."

Then the Spirit of God reminded me of Luke 15, in which Jesus tells the story that we have come to know as the Parable of the Prodigal Son. God impressed upon me that the father in this parable extended gentle love and welcome to both of his sons who were lost in different ways. One was the prodigal son, who had run away from home and indulged in wild living until it left him starving and broken—a young man not unlike William. When he returned home, the father ran to him, reestablished his place in the family and community, and orchestrated a lavish party to welcome him back. The other son was the prodigal's elder brother, who stayed home but resented his work and place in the family. He was duty-bound yet unloving and wanted no part in bringing the stinking runaway back into the family fold—a man not unlike Church Guy.

As I got out of my car and walked into our home, I remembered the father's words from the parable: "All I have is yours. And we have to celebrate!" This was the invitation he gave to *both* sons to receive grace, forgiveness, welcome, and celebration. We receive this same gentle invitation from our heavenly Father. Both the lawbreakers and the law-bound can be lost and can be found. And it is the gentleness of Christ that brings them both together—prodigals and Pharisees, junkies and Church Guys—to bring them, and us, home.

QUESTIONS FOR REFLECTION AND DISCUSSION

1. Name one thing from this chapter that troubled you, inspired you, or both. Why were you impacted in this way?
2. Between William and Church Guy, who do you identify with most easily? Why do you think Church Guys are so put off by people like William? Which of the two is most likely to have a deep affection for Jesus, and why?
3. How can political conservatism damage the witness of the gospel? How can political liberalism damage the witness

of the gospel? How should we be addressing this reality in our faith communities and in our own lives? In what ways are we most susceptible to conflating politics with faith? Why is doing so unwise?

4. Based on this chapter, identify one way that the Lord might be nudging you toward growth or change. What steps should you take to pursue the change?

THREE

He Disarms the Cynic in Us

For some people, it is hard to love Jesus. The reasons can be deeply personal and emotional.

For example, my father, now in his mid-seventies, bristles with something resembling a post-traumatic twitch whenever we bring up Jesus to him in conversation. Why is this so? Because he was raised in a church that would make most people want to become an atheist. The church's message was filled with shaming, scolding, and hellfire. Moral expectations were impossibly high and delivered from the pulpit in a "Do as I say, not as I do" fashion. The grace, love, and kindness of God toward sinners was rarely if ever mentioned. Add to this a verbally abusive, difficult mother whose private life was utterly incongruent with her public persona of a virtuous woman, and the likelihood of a man coming to believe in and surrender his life to Jesus becomes highly unlikely. Ever since my brother and I became followers of Christ, we've been trying to persuade Dad that the portrait of Jesus he grew up with looks almost nothing like the Jesus of the gentle answer—the Jesus who actually *is*. So far, even though Dad is warm to our commitment to faith, our persuasive efforts in his case have been to no avail. Please pray that someday and somehow, the truth will break through.

I think also of an atheist friend of mine who is angry at the God he says he believes does not exist. Once I asked him why he is so hostile toward the idea of God and especially toward the God of Christianity, and his answer left me speechless. "If I'm being honest," my friend responded, "my issues with Jesus aren't intellectual. I am actually of the belief that it takes more faith *not* to believe in God than it does to believe in him. My real problem is that Jesus is a forgiving man, and if I follow Jesus it means I will have to become a forgiving man also. And I simply can't imagine the horrific pain it would cause me to have to forgive my father for the things he did to me."

Much like Jonah's angry reaction to God's intention to be gracious, kind, and forgiving to the brutal Ninevites—a people who were known by Jonah and the Israelites to be violent, bloodthirsty, power-hungry bullies and aggressors—my atheist friend could not envision himself bearing the cost of injuries that had been perpetrated toward *him* by the man who was supposed to *protect* him from injury. "What kind of God would let a bully get off scot-free and then insist that the victims extend forgiveness?" If you've ever been a victim of abuse, I'm sure you understand the struggle.

And then there is Holly,[1] a woman in her early twenties who occasionally slips into the back row of the balcony of our church on Sundays. Recently, Holly asked to meet with me in my office to discuss a personal struggle of hers. Her posture was what seemed to be a combination of warmth, respect, and anxiety, all bunched up together. The warmth and respect came from the woman that she is—a kindhearted, loving, inquisitive, sensitive, tender soul. The anxiety came from what she saw as a conflict between her sexuality and her faith. On the one hand, she was in a relationship with a woman whom she described as the love of her life and a person she could not envision having to live without. On the other hand, she knew her Bible well, which told her in no uncertain terms that her love was not to be acted upon, leaving her with what seemed to be an impossible choice. "Is Jesus asking me to choose between *her* and *him*?" she asked me through tears. "If he is, then how could he put me and so many others in such an impossible position? I never asked to be attracted to women. I never wanted to fall in love with a woman. And yet I have. And I also love Jesus, or at least I *want* to love him. But it seems that he is putting me in a position to have to choose between two loves. How can he do this to me?"

And then there is the fictional story that isn't really fiction to so many veterans of war—the story of Lieutenant Dan Taylor in the blockbuster movie *Forrest Gump.* After having his legs blown off in Vietnam, Lieutenant Dan is dependent on "the system" for his care and survival rather than living as the independent, self-sufficient man he once was. His anger, despair, and bitterness overflow in a conversation with his friend Forrest.

"Have you found Jesus yet, Gump?" asked Lieutenant Dan.

"I didn't know I was supposed to be looking for him, sir," Forrest responded.

Lieutenant Dan chuckles dryly, then says, "That's all these

cripples down at the VA ever talk about: Jesus this and Jesus that. Have I found Jesus? They even had a priest come and talk to me. He said God is listening, but I have to help myself, and if I accept Jesus in my heart, then I'll get to walk beside him in the kingdom of heaven." Lieutenant Dan throws a bottle, then shouts, "Did you hear what I said? *Walk* beside him in the kingdom of heaven! Well, kiss my crippled a—. God is listening? What a crock of s—t."[2]

These two encounters, actual and fictional, are representative of the perspective of many who keep their distance from God and especially from Jesus.

The Bible has its share of such people keeping their distance from God too. When Adam and Eve heard the voice of God in the garden, they both hid and covered themselves for fear of being exposed in their nakedness and shame (Gen. 3:8). Ashamed of his life and friendless, Zacchaeus doesn't presume to approach Jesus for friendship. Instead, he climbs up into a tree to observe Jesus from a distance (Luke 19:1–10). Impaired by guilt and shame, when Peter encounters the teaching and power of Jesus, he says to the Lord, "Depart from me, for I am a sinful man, O Lord" (Luke 5:8). To such people, and to many of us, the presence and favor of the Lord seems inaccessible due to the gap between God's glory, loveliness, and holiness and the stain of human shame and sin.

And then there were the scribes and Pharisees, who distanced themselves from Jesus for different reasons. They presumed to be *better* than him and resented him for his growing influence and popularity (John 11:48). These Pharisees endeavored to do away with Jesus by discrediting him (Luke 7:39), attempting to throw him off a cliff (Luke 4:29), and eventually begging the governor, Pilate, to crucify him (Matt. 27:22).

THE RELUCTANT, OPPOSITIONAL DISCIPLE

Even Nathanael, who would become one of Jesus' twelve disciples and eventually give up his life as a martyr for the cause of Christ, began his relationship with Jesus on shaky ground. We might say that Nathanael, upon being introduced to Jesus by his friend, Philip, responded to the Lord with a lack of gentleness. Instead, Nathanael responded to Jesus—and especially to the claim Philip was making that he was the Messiah foretold in the Old Testament scriptures, who had now come into the world—with cynicism and skepticism. The account is told as follows:

> Jesus decided to go to Galilee. He found Philip and said to him, "Follow me." Now Philip was from Bethsaida, the city of Andrew and Peter. Philip found Nathanael and said to him, "We have found him of whom Moses in the Law and also the prophets wrote, Jesus of Nazareth, the son of Joseph." Nathanael said to him, "Can anything good come out of Nazareth?" Philip said to him, "Come and see." Jesus saw Nathanael coming toward him and said of him, "Behold, an Israelite indeed, in whom there is no deceit!" Nathanael said to him, "How do you know me?" Jesus answered him, "Before Philip called you, when you were under the fig tree, I saw you." Nathanael answered him, "Rabbi, you are the Son of God! You are the King of Israel!" Jesus answered him, "Because I said to you, 'I saw you under the fig tree,' do you believe? You will see greater things than these." And he said to him, "Truly, truly, I say to you, you will see heaven opened, and the angels of God ascending and descending on the Son of Man." (John 1:43–51)

Here we see that Nathanael's reasons for keeping his distance from Jesus were many and revealed in the beginning a reluctant, if not oppositional, posture in his heart toward Jesus.

For Social Reasons

First, he distanced himself from Jesus for *social* reasons. When Philip came to Nathanael and said, "We have found him of whom Moses . . . and also the prophets wrote, Jesus of Nazareth, the son of Joseph," Nathanael famously replied, "Can anything good come out of Nazareth?" The question is rhetorical, and the presumed answer is no.

Nazareth, far from being a city of movers and shakers, was known as a city of underdogs and losers. To the average person in those days, Nazareth was regarded (or, better said, disregarded) as a small, obscure, irrelevant, on-the-fringes hick town. It would never cross the mind of any first-century Jewish man that the Messiah would or *could* originate from such a place. Jerusalem or Judea, perhaps. But Nazareth? No way. And yet it was indeed Nazareth that God selected and appointed as the place out of which his Son, the King of the world—and the One who would come to make all things new through his life, death, burial, resurrection, and coming return in power and majesty and glory (Rev. 21:1–7)—would first make his entry as a man on the global and cosmic scene.

A careful reading of Scripture reveals that this is God's preferred way to make his presence known on earth—not chiefly through movers, shakers, and A-listers, but rather through outcasts, losers, those of ill repute, and those who were held in low esteem. If we examine Jesus' friendships, for example, we will notice a disproportionately low number of celebrities, powerful politicians, affluent business people, high-society people, prominent leaders, and the like. But if you were a known prostitute or a tax collector, an addict or an alcoholic, a no-name, a leper or paralytic, or a despised and rejected sinner, your chances of being invited into Jesus' inner circle of friends would increase.

So scandalous and unexpected were Jesus' associations that he was accused of being a glutton, a drunk, and a friend of tax collectors and sinners (Luke 7:34). The scribes and Pharisees shamed, scolded, and excluded such sinners for their failure to measure up. Yet these strugglers experienced Jesus as humble, gentle, and kind—attributes the scribes and Pharisees knew little to nothing about, because they were too busy separating the world between the good people and the bad people, the saints and the sinners, the virtuous and the scumbags, the insiders and the outsiders, the worthy and the unworthy. Meanwhile, Jesus was hanging out with, befriending, and welcoming religious society's choice rejects, thereby separating the world between the proud and the humble.

Have you ever met a person who says they fell in love with Jesus because a religious person or group of religious people scolded them for their morals, their ethics, and their lifestyle choices? In all my years, I have yet to meet a man, woman, or child with such a story. But among the thousands of Christians that I do know, there are more than I could count who fell in love with Jesus because of the gentleness of Christ, as expressed to them through Christians.

Nathanael's "Can anything good come out of Nazareth" response is rooted in what we might call a judgment trigger. Judgment triggers are those criteria we use to separate the world between the good and the bad, the in and the out, us and them. We see this dynamic in the parable of the Pharisee and the tax collector that Jesus relates in Luke 18. Jesus tells of two men praying in the temple. The first, the Pharisee, says, "God, I thank you that I am not like other men, extortioners, unjust, adulterers, or even like this tax collector. I fast twice a week; I give tithes of all that I get" (vv. 11–12). The second, the tax collector, stands far off and in humility won't even lift his eyes toward heaven. Instead, and without a shred of perceivable judgment or scorn in his heart toward the Pharisee praying against him, simply prays, "God, be merciful to me, the sinner!" (v. 13). Jesus condemns the smug, scolding Pharisee and acquits the contrite tax collector. He will never despise a broken and contrite heart (Ps. 51:7). He opposes the proud, but gives grace to the humble (James 4:6).

Too often, we are like the Pharisee in Jesus' parable. We believe that we are righteous, and as a result we treat other people with contempt. Our judgment triggers—those corrupt and smug places in the soul that ask questions like, "Can anything good come out of . . . ?" and that pray prayers like, "Thank you, my God, that I am not like other men"—are the various ism's we latch onto for our own sense of value and worth and rightness and self-justification and better-than-ness in the world. Our potential ism's, the ones by which we judge as well as the ones because of which we resent others for judging us, are many: tribalism, racism, sexism, nationalism, conservatism, liberalism, classism, Wesleyanism, Calvinism (one assumes that Wesley and Calvin, both humble men, would have rejected the idea of *ism* being attached to their names), and the list goes on.

Thankfully, Jesus didn't share or abide by any of the socially exclusive ism's to which we are often bound. What's more, he would have been excluded by most such measures. Those of us who measure a person's worth by dollars instead of dignity would do well to remember that Jesus couldn't afford a place to live (Matt. 8:20). Those of us who measure a person's potential by where she went to college should note that Jesus didn't go to college or to school at all (John 7:15). Those of us who measure a person's significance by their line of work ought to recall that Jesus worked with his hands (Mark 6:3). Those of us who measure a person's beauty by his external appearance should observe that Jesus was average looking at best, if not outright unattractive (Isa. 53:2). Those of us who determine whether or not we want to befriend a person on the basis of his popularity or the types of associations that he keeps should remember that Jesus was a man of no reputation, even his own people did not receive him, and he was chiefly seen as a friend to sinners (John 1:11; Matt. 11:16–19). And those of us who measure a person's desirability by his marital and familial status ought not forget that Jesus had no wife and no children.

Given all the characteristics that would place Jesus on the fringes of so many circles, is it any wonder that Nathanael and those like him might ask the question, "Can anything good come out of . . . ?"

For Political Reasons

A second reason Nathanael and others may have distanced themselves from Jesus is *political*. Like every other Jewish male, Nathanael would have been steeped in the Old Testament scriptures that predicted a Messiah who would one day come and assume rule and reign over the entire world. As Isaiah foretold about the coming Messiah:

> For to us a child is born,
> to us a son is given;

and the government shall be upon his shoulder,
and his name shall be called
Wonderful Counselor, Mighty God,
Everlasting Father, Prince of Peace.
Of the increase of his government and of peace
there will be no end,
on the throne of David and over his kingdom,
to establish it and to uphold it
with justice and with righteousness
from this time forth and forevermore.
The zeal of the Lord of hosts will do this. (Isa. 9:6–7)

The interpretation of such scriptures that prevailed in first-century Palestine did not picture a Savior coming from a small, obscure town, or in a quiet way, or being rejected and killed. Rather, the prevailing vision was for something resembling the exodus event so that, through the leadership of a prophet like Moses, Israel would once again be delivered from violent, oppressive, enslaving rule. The notion of a gentle deliverer—of One who loves his enemies instead of destroying them, of One who endeavors to bring reconciliation between not only a holy God and sinful people but between those people themselves—seemed inconceivable.

Rather than anticipating a Messiah who would bring peace to *all* the world spiritually, socially, and culturally, Nathanael and most others anticipated an absolute ruler. They were looking for a military and political champion, one with optics similar to those of King Saul, a decorated warrior who "was taller than any of the people" (1 Sam. 9:2). They were looking for a man of muscle, a Nietszchean *Übermensch* to lead them and to fight for them.[3] They were looking for a leader who would ultimately put the likes of Nebuchadnezzar's Babylon, Caesar's Rome, and the Nineveh of Jonah's day in their dreadful, well-deserved, decisively and eternally defeated place.

Yet what was Nathanael told instead? That a no-name from Nazareth—the son of two poor refugee teenagers—had come to rule the world.

Had Nathanael seen the Broadway musical *Jesus Christ, Superstar,* he might have sympathized with the snarky words from its Pontius Pilate: "Who is this broken man cluttering up my hallway? Who is this unfortunate? . . . so this is Jesus Christ, I am really quite surprised. You look so small—not a king at all."[4]

For Personal Reasons

Lastly, there was a *personal* reason why Nathanael might keep his distance from Jesus—Jesus was getting too close. In response to the young man's insult, Jesus shockingly replied, "Behold, an Israelite indeed, in whom there is no deceit" (John 1:47).

This simple and complimentary remark about Nathanael's personality felt too close for comfort, so the walls went up. You might say that he shared the view of Jean-Paul Sartre's Garcin in *No Exit,* who complained, "Hell is—other people!"[5] For Nathanael, it seems, Jesus is too much of a close-talker, and perhaps an invader of personal space and privacy. As a defense mechanism, Nathanael responds with an air of bravado, asking what appears to be a scorning question, "How do *you* [a person from Nazareth] know *me*?" (John 1:48, emphasis mine).

THE GENTLE, PATIENT JESUS WHO SEES US

Yet almost immediately after throwing up these walls, Nathanael does an immediate about-face, a decisive and repentant turn toward Jesus, acknowledging that Jesus is the Son of God and King of Israel (John 1:49). What triggers his turn? Note that it occurs in response to an odd comment from Jesus: "Before Philip called you, when you were under the fig tree, I saw you" (v. 48).

From the moment Jesus utters these strange words, it is game over for Nathanael. The snubbing posture is suddenly gone, with no more distancing himself from Jesus. Instead, he calls Jesus *Rabbi*, a term Jewish men would use to convey respect and esteem and to signal that they were eager and ready to build their entire lives around the rabbi's teaching and vision. Nathanael goes even further, saying, "You are the Son of God! You are the King of Israel" (v. 49).

Why did this Nathanael—a disrespectful social and political and personal cynic just a moment before—suddenly declare absolute belief in and allegiance toward Jesus? I believe the answer lies in something Jesus says to Nathanael, implicitly and explicitly, three times in the course of their conversation: "I saw you."

What was it that Jesus *saw* when he observed Nathanael under the fig tree? We can only speculate because scripture is silent, but we can assume that it was something very personal to Nathanael. We also know that the way Jesus handled what he saw changed the entire trajectory and demeanor of Nathanael's life. Whatever it was, being seen and then affirmed by Jesus hit Nathanael at an emotional, visceral, and perhaps extraordinarily vulnerable level. Wherever our imaginations may take us, Jesus' treatment of Nathanael affirms two things about Jesus, the gentle Savior: he sees both the best and the worst in us, and he loves us just the same. Let's examine both of these truths.

Jesus Sees the Best in Us

It should not be lost on us that, in Nathanael's case, Jesus did not respond to insult with injury. In response to Nathanael's "Can anything good come from . . . ?" and "How do *you* know *me*?" talk, Jesus did not retaliate nor did he even seem to get offended. Instead, Jesus responded with a gentle answer laden with kindness, humility, and charity: "You, sir, are a man in whom there is no deceit!"

This is not how I respond to insults. If someone insults me on the Internet, I might respond with a zinger of my own (on a bad day) or by clicking on the Block button (on a good day). The self-protective, fight-or-flight instinct feels so natural to me that it's almost like breathing. When I feel I am being criticized or attacked, even by remote strangers, my first impulse can be to go on the defense. "How dare he criticize me like this! Who does she think she is?" When the defensiveness rises up, it reveals how little I actually believe the gospel, which tells me that in Jesus I am not condemned, that all my guilt and wrongness has been taken care of at the cross, and that the adopting smile of God hovers over me always. Somehow, the cosmic, unshakable truths about my identity in Christ get lost in the noise of even a small, petty, relatively insignificant critique. My fragile ego has been bruised; therefore, I must self-protect by striking back or by blowing off the critic.

And if someone insults me to my face, even when done playfully or jokingly, it can be even worse . . .

Once, when I was traveling with my wife, Patti, and our two daughters on a New York subway train, a disheveled, drunk woman approached us and paid a compliment to Patti. "Your girls," she said, "are sooooooo beautiful! You must be so proud of them!"

"Yes, I am. Thank you," Patti replied.

The woman looked over at me and continued, "I'll bet Grandpa over here is really proud of them too!"

Even though the woman was only teasing, I wanted to make her pay with an insult—one that employed my verbal comeback skills and my sobriety advantage—that would cut the woman down to size. Instead, I bit my tongue, waited until we got off the train, and then said to my family, "Can you believe the nerve of that woman?" They all just looked at me with grins on their faces, almost like a wink to remind me of my receding hairline, eye wrinkles, and all the other signs of age. I relaxed, we moved on, and I remember praying at some later point for the drunk woman we met on the train—that God would have compassion on her and deal kindly with her. Only God knows what kind of story it was that got her to that place.

But Jesus didn't need a grin or a wink to respond with gentleness and compassion to Nathanael. Instead, there was an immediate affirmation, a gesture of gentleness and love and mercy and kindness: "Behold! A man in whom there is no deceit!" It was as if Jesus was saying something like, "There's an integrity I see in you, Nathanael . . . one that, perhaps, Philip and others aren't as easily able to see. You are a truth-teller with an honest heart. You never leave us guessing, do you?"

Then Jesus referred to a section from the Old Testament that Nathanael would have been very familiar with: Genesis 28, where

God uses the image of angels climbing up and down a ladder to communicate to the patriarch Jacob that his access to God would be free and readily available from that point forward, as if he had his own personal pipeline to heaven. What's more, God promised to Jacob a land resembling heaven itself—something akin to a new heaven and a new earth coming down out of heaven from God (Rev. 21:1–7). He would turn Jacob into the spiritual father of all of God's children. Jacob's response to this God-given vision is similar to Nathanael's enthusiastic response to Jesus. "How awesome is this place!" Jacob said.

Let's not miss a significant detail. In Hebrew, the name Jacob means *liar.* When he was born, Jacob's biological father named him with a curse instead of a blessing. Yet later, Jacob's Maker and Redeemer, the Creator of things as great as stars and galaxies and as mundane as toenails and nose hairs, gave him a different name with a different purpose. "From now on," he said to Jacob, "your name will be Israel." Israel was a name that described how Jacob had wrestled with God and prevailed. The unloved son, who all his life had been marked by a curse from his father, became the recipient of the greatest paternal blessing of all—the blessing of being renamed and repurposed by Yahweh, the God and Father of the Lord Jesus Christ and the Father of all who come to know Jesus as Rabbi.

Jacob was deceitful. Nathanael was abrasive. Yet both of them received a blessing instead of a curse. From the same divine lips, Jacob was no longer called a liar and Nathanael was called a truth-teller. Isn't such kindness almost too much to take in?

In Cormac McCarthy's novel *No Country for Old Men*, the aging and fatigued and retired sheriff says to his uncle, "I always thought when I got older that God would sort of come into my life in some way. He didn't. I don't blame him. If I was him I would have the same opinion about me that he does."[6]

Yet as Yahweh's response to Jacob and Jesus' answer to Nathanael reveal, the sheriff has the wrong opinion about God, for God delights in grace toward his children. He doesn't define us by our worst behavior or the terrible names given to us by others. Instead, Jacob is the prevailing wrestler and Nathanael is the honest man. Other examples abound. There's the inconsistent, unpredictable disciple, Peter, who Jesus names Rock (Matt. 16:18). There's the poor widow who gives a small sum of money who Jesus calls the most generous person of all (Luke 21:1–4). There's the prostitute who barges in uninvited to a Pharisee's dinner party and, using the tools of her trade (her lips, her hair, and her perfume), she demonstrates public affection to Jesus in the only ways she knows how. Most of the guests at the party call her a sinner and treat her like an animal instead of a human, a thing instead of a person, yet Jesus calls her exemplary, for having been forgiven much, she has also loved much (Luke 7:36–50).

The point is this: *all of these were undeserving people whose lives were utterly transformed by the gentleness of their God.*

He Sees the Worst in Us

As it is with Nathanael and the others, so it is with us. When those he has called to himself fight against him, he responds by fighting *for* us . . . and for our hearts. His chief strategy is to return our insults with his kindness, our persecution with his prayers, our dismissive attitudes with his attentiveness, and our brashness with his kindness. As the Proverbs make clear, "A gentle answer turns away wrath" (Prov. 15:1 NIV).

So what *was* it that Jesus saw when he saw Nathanael under

a fig tree? It could have been something wonderful, like a hidden virtue. Perhaps Nathanael had been praying under the tree, or making a vow, or feeding a hungry man, or defending a weaker person against a bully, or donating new clothes to a poor woman, or talking a teenager out of committing suicide, or forgiving an enemy.

Or Jesus could have seen hidden pain in Nathanael under that fig tree. Perhaps it was the place where Nathanael first became a victim of abuse, cried out to a silent sky about how lonely he was, or tried to take his own life, or felt the despair of anxiety or depression or financial ruin, or was given a crippling diagnosis, or was abandoned by his wife, or buried a child.

Or Jesus could have seen Nathanael committing a heinous sin that was hidden from the rest of the world. Perhaps beneath the fig tree was where Nathanael berated and bullied a child, or committed a crime, or passed out drunk, or told an injurious lie, or committed a murder, or solicited a prostitute, or committed blasphemy.

"EVEN GREATER THINGS THAN THESE"

We just don't know what Jesus observed in that moment. However, when Nathanael responded in awe over the fact that Jesus had seen him under the fig tree, Jesus assured him that the best was still to come: "You will see greater things than these." The greater thing to which Jesus referred was that Nathanael, like Jacob, would see heaven opened and the angels of God ascending and descending on the Son of Man (vv. 50–51). In other words, Nathanael would see the face of God, in all of his glory and splendor.

Philip, the friend who first introduced Nathanael to Jesus, was also promised greater things. When Philip later asked Jesus to "show us the Father," Jesus responded, "Truly, truly, I say to you, whoever believes in me will also do the works that I do; and greater works than these will he do" (John 14:12).

What are these greater works that Jesus spoke of? What could be an even greater work than turning water into wine, walking on water, telling a paralytic to rise up and walk, or giving sight to a blind man? Perhaps the greater works are things such as Nathanael the cynic becoming a loyal follower who calls Jesus Rabbi, or a wavering Peter doing something courageous and bold, or a poor widow giving away her two coins at the temple, or a violent and racist Saul becoming a reconciling mediator between Jews and Gentiles.

Perhaps greater works are the works done in our own lives through Jesus' strength, such as loving one person for better and for worse, in sickness and in health, in joy and in sorrow, as long as we both shall live. Perhaps greater works include saying no to a doctor's recommendation to abort a child with special needs and yes to raising and loving that child. Perhaps greater works include pursuing understanding, reconciliation, justice, peace, and friendship with people from another race, culture, political persuasion, economic group, or generation whom you wouldn't otherwise be able to get along with outside of Christ. Perhaps greater works include staying at the same church for years or even decades, even during seasons of difficulty or decline. Or perhaps greater works include responding to injurious treatment with a gentle answer that turns away wrath.

In the fall of 2006, a Pennsylvania milk truck driver named Charles Carl Roberts IV burst into a one-room Amish schoolhouse and opened fire on a classroom of girls, killing five and severely injuring five more. After this, he turned the gun on himself and took his own life.

In his suicide note, Mr. Roberts confessed that he had been secretly tormented for many years by two dark spots from his own past. The first was the memory of how he had molested two of his younger relatives twenty years before. The second was the memory of losing his own daughter, who had died nine years previously. The loss of his child led Mr. Roberts to also confess in his note that he hated God.

There were two groups of people in attendance at his funeral. The first was the expected group: his family and friends of his family, who sat somber and shocked over what had happened. The second was a group of about thirty men, women, and children from the Amish community whose daughters Roberts had murdered and injured. Commenting on the series of events, nearby sociologist and college professor Donald Kraybull remarked that "the most powerful demonstration of the depth of Amish forgiveness was when members of the Amish community went to the killer's burial service . . . Several families, Amish families who had buried their own daughters just the day before were in attendance and they hugged the widow, and hugged other members of the killer's family." It was also reported that this Amish community had donated money to cover expenses, including funeral costs, for the killer's widow and three children. Then, as would be the case for any community after enduring such horrific loss, the Amish returned home where they would be "better able to concentrate on the work of their own healing."[7]

When I first read this modern-day account of "greater works than these," I couldn't help but remember the famous quote from Dr. Martin Luther King Jr. as he eloquently explained the rationale behind his philosophy of protesting injustice by acts of *peaceful* resistance. King said, "Returning violence for violence multiplies violence, adding deeper darkness to a night already devoid of stars. Darkness cannot drive out darkness: only light can do that. Hate cannot drive out hate: only love can do that."[8] This is a gift of love packaged in a gentle yet powerful answer.

How do imperfect, frail human beings find the resources to distancing and rejection, to respond to such violence with such love, and to commit to "work on their own healing" instead of retaliating with their own forms of aggression?

I believe the answer rests in a short statement made by the beloved disciple, John, who said that we love (even our enemies) because Jesus first loved us (1 John 4:19). Paul, likewise, reminds us that we only have the resources to forgive others because Christ has first forgiven us (Eph. 4:32).

To gain strength and courage to offer a gentle answer, we must first be flooded by the reality that we've already received one.

QUESTIONS FOR REFLECTION AND DISCUSSION

1. Name one thing from this chapter that troubled you, inspired you, or both. Why were you impacted in this way?
2. Nathanael distanced himself from Jesus for social, political, and personal reasons. Which of these three reasons—social, political, and personal—is the most prominent reason why people distance themselves from

Jesus today? Which of the three tempts you the most to keep your own distance, and why?

3. Do you believe that Jesus Christ "sees" you in the same way that he saw Nathanael under the tree? If so, how does this awareness impact your affections and receptivity toward him? How does it impact your response to those who seem to want to distance themselves from you?
4. Based on this chapter, identify one way that the Lord might be nudging you toward growth or change. What steps should you take to pursue the change?

PART II

HOW HIS GENTLENESS CHANGES US

You have given me the shield of your salvation, and your right hand supported me, and your gentleness made me great.

—Psalm 18:35

FOUR

We Grow Thicker Skin

If we want to follow Jesus, we'll need to adjust our expectations for the life he gives us. Especially in the West, our vision for the good life includes what the United States Declaration of Independence calls a "self-evident" truth that all people are endowed by our Creator with "unalienable Rights" that include "Life, Liberty and the pursuit of Happiness."[1]

When life, liberty, and happiness are viewed through a biblical lens, Christians especially can and should embrace this declaration with gusto. However, when defined by a modern Western point of view, our understanding of the phrase can potentially stand in opposition with Jesus' own vision for the good life. Jesus was a man of sorrows, acquainted with grief, whose own life did not square at all with the so-called American Dream. He lived much of his life in poverty, was maligned and misunderstood, was an embarrassment to his own family members, was betrayed by his closest friends, and was brutally executed in his early thirties by Roman authorities. Furthermore, Jesus declared that all who follow him must lose their lives in order to find them, and they must deny themselves daily and take up a cross just as he did.

Jesus is not opposed to happiness. Far from it! In fact, the world he created and that will be again—as pictured in the garden of Eden and the new heaven and new earth—is a world filled with *nothing but* deep happiness. The promise of a perfectly restored Eden existence has been declared and made possible by Jesus, yet we await this full provision. In the waiting we see glimpses of future glory and peace that will come, yet the world we live in is presently broken. In this world of the already but not yet, Jesus is often at odds with our typical ideas about the *basis* for happiness. In the West, we tend to expect things like a loving marriage, a stable family, supportive friends, a satisfying job, a secure financial situation, a nice house, and an admirable reputation to make us happy. We believe that being happy is the equivalent of being successful, comfortable, and in control of our lives. While there is nothing wrong with these things in themselves, according to Jesus we should take great care not to depend upon them as our reasons for being happy. Nor should their presence in our lives cause us to assume that we are necessarily flourishing.

For those of us who are Christians and who live in this place we call "the land of the free and the home of the brave," we must reconcile our assumed vision of the good life with something Jesus said would be true for every one of his followers:

> Blessed are those who are persecuted for righteousness' sake, for theirs is the kingdom of heaven. Blessed are you when others revile you and persecute you and utter all kinds of evil against you falsely on my account. Rejoice and be glad, for your

> reward is great in heaven, for so they persecuted the prophets who were before you. (Matt. 5:10–12)

Surprisingly, the word translated *blessed* in this passage is the Greek equivalent of our English word *happy.* Jesus is saying that the happiest, most well-adjusted, peace-filled people are those who will sometimes take it on the chin because of their belief and love for him. The happy people will be those who are persecuted, slandered, sucker-punched, excluded, and bullied because of their connection with Jesus Christ.

Sounds fun, doesn't it? So . . . who's in?

A NECESSARY PARADIGM SHIFT

Christians in the West must understand that the relative ease of our experience following Christ is unusual. The freedoms, comforts, and safety we enjoy make us like unicorns to most of our brothers and sisters throughout history and around the world today. Even as I write this, Sri Lankan Christians are recovering from a recent terrorist bombing on their churches. In the Easter Sunday attack, more than two hundred men, women, and children lost their lives and hundreds of others were injured and hospitalized. Similarly, the Chinese government is cracking down on Christian houses of worship, forbidding pastors to preach Christ as Scripture presents him, and threatening separation from their families and imprisonment if they do not comply.

In December 2018, CNN reported that more than one hundred Christians had been detained in China for the crime of "inciting subversion of state power."[2] One such detainee was

Rev. Wang Yi, pastor of one of China's many thriving, underground house churches. In response to his imprisonment, Yi wrote and publicized an open letter he called "My Declaration of Faithful Disobedience." In that letter, he said:

> I have no fear of any social or political power. For the Bible teaches us that God establishes governmental authorities in order to terrorize evildoers, not to terrorize doers of good . . . this [is] the very reason why the Communist regime is filled with fear at a church that is no longer afraid of it . . . Those who lock me up will one day be locked up by angels. Those who interrogate me will finally be questioned and judged by Christ . . . Separate me from my wife and children, ruin my reputation, destroy my life and my family . . . authorities are capable of doing all of these things. However, no one can force me to renounce my faith.[3]

Meanwhile, as our brothers and sisters across the globe expect and experience violence, oppression, and death, we in the West get our feelings hurt, withdraw from people relationally, and even become hostile when someone mildly criticizes us for our faith. We can be thankful for the religious freedoms we enjoy and for the relatively safe world in which we live. However, the contrast between the depths of life-threatening persecution and the shallows of social media criticism should provide us with needed biblical perspective. Truth be told, we have it relatively easy in the West, which means that we should not become as easily offended as we often do.

Jesus warned his disciples, "If the world hates you, know that it has hated me before it hated you. If you were of the world, the world would love you as its own; but because you are not of the world, but I chose you out of the world, therefore the world hates you . . . If they persecuted me, they will also persecute you . . . [a]nd you also will bear witness" (John 15:18, 20, 27).

Jesus' deeper warning rings out as we remember that the word *witness* comes from the Greek word meaning *martyr*. Indeed, the ordinary experience of bearing witness to Jesus includes not only mild and occasional criticism, but also opposition, slander, aggression, hatred, and even death.

This reality of religious persecution traces back to Israel's enslavement by the Egyptian Pharaoh, under whose reign God's people were oppressed, mischaracterized, and forced by an iron fist to manufacture bricks without straw. The Old Testament prophets continued the theme as Israel was conquered, pillaged, and tortured by more powerful pagan nations who forced them into further exile and enslavement. The entire New Testament was brought into the world by an oppressed and mistreated people, who were labeled as insubordinate enemies of the state because of their open belief that Jesus, not the Roman Caesar, was Lord. Every time we open our Bibles, we must remember that almost every word was written by someone who was tortured, imprisoned, a refugee in hiding, or some combination thereof. The apostle Paul was beaten, arrested, and unjustly incarcerated for his faith. He wrote Ephesians, Philippians, Colossians, and Philemon from prison. Ten of the twelve disciples died as martyrs for committing the crime of preaching the gospel. (Judas took his own life after betraying Jesus, and John died of old age while imprisoned on a remote island.)

Miraculously, the persecution and martyrdom of the earliest Christian leaders led to explosive growth of the Christian movement and of the church herself. As the church father Tertullian famously said, "The blood of the martyrs is the seed of the Church."[4]

We must remember that systemic, pervasive persecution of Christian believers is not merely an ancient reality. Today, more than 75 percent of the world's population lives in societies that impose severe religious restrictions. Christians in more than sixty countries experience persecution from their governments and their neighbors. Each month 322 Christians are killed, 214 churches and Christian properties are destroyed, and 772 forms of violence such as forced marriages, rape, beatings, and arrest are perpetrated globally against believers in Christ.[5]

These realities, both ancient and modern, raise some soul-searching questions for Christians who reside in the so-called land of the free and home of the brave. Do we really know what it means to be free? Do we truly understand what it takes to be brave? What does it mean for us who believe that it is every person's self-evident, unalienable right to have life, liberty, and the pursuit of happiness? Should the fact that we are spared from life-threatening persecution be a source of guilt and shame for us? Or should this be a cause for gratitude? What does this all mean for us, and how should it impact our posture in a Western society that is so characterized by us-against-them?

OUR RESPONSIBILITY IN A WORLD WHERE PERSECUTION IS REAL

When Jesus said that the persecuted are blessed, he added to this the declaration that "*theirs* is the kingdom of heaven" (Matt. 5:10, emphasis mine). As their fellow heirs, those of us who experience relatively low levels of persecution ought to consider how we can support and provide care for those who bear the weight of this unique form of suffering. Our call from the Lord is both a call to justice and a call to courage.

A Call to Justice

In addition to our call to expect persecution for our faith, Christians are also called to be among the world's foremost leaders in the defense and protection of persecuted classes of people. This includes the unborn, the poor, the marginalized, oppressed minorities, as well as religious believers—whether Christian, Jewish, Muslim, or otherwise—who are persecuted for their faith. We have been commissioned by our Lord to stand for all of the world's weak, vulnerable, and oppressed.[6] We are indeed called to a form of *anger* that, while never retaliatory or vindictive in nature, is nonetheless righteous and proactive and protective. (We will explore this in greater depth in the next chapter.)

Jesus revealed his own posture toward religious persecution in the violent killing of Stephen, history's first recorded Christian martyr. The story is told in Acts 7:54–8:3, in which Saul of Tarsus, who would later convert to Christianity and become the apostle Paul, presides over Stephen's torturous death. Stephen, a man described as being "full of grace and power," preaches the gospel in a public place. As enraged people in power prepare to kill him by hurling rocks at his head, Stephen looks toward heaven and prays that God would forgive them. As he does, he also catches a glimpse of Jesus *standing* at the right hand of God in heaven. By this time, the work of Jesus on the cross (his own martyrdom) and through the resurrection was complete. Because his mission had been accomplished, scripture says that Jesus *sat down* at God's right hand, resting and satisfied from his work (Mark 16:19). Yet Stephen saw Jesus take a *standing*, proactive posture to defend him and his cause. It's as if Jesus is saying with his body language, "That's my boy. With him I am well pleased. And there will come a time when I will rise up in my return to vindicate him, as well as all who experience opposition, scorn, hatred, mocking, slander, mistreatment, and torture for my name's sake."

In consideration of the call of justice, which beckons us to defend and vindicate the weak and oppressed and persecuted, Jewish Holocaust victim and human rights activist Elie Wiesel said in his Nobel Peace Prize speech, "Whenever men and women are persecuted because of their race, religion, or political views, that place must—at that moment—become the center of the universe."[7]

Bishop N. T. Wright declared that Christians especially "are responsible, before God, to exercise justice . . . to defend the vulnerable. When leaders fail to do this, it is the role of the people of God to remind them, through critique, through noncollaboration, and if necessary, through martyrdom."[8]

Whenever and wherever there is persecution, opposition, or unjust treatment of vulnerable persons, Christians are called by God to serve as the conscience of society by speaking truth to power. Perhaps in the land of the free and home of the brave, this ought to be a Christian's primary way to follow Jesus in a world where others routinely suffer for their faith.

A Call to Courage

Speaking truth to power is a valiant endeavor. It is also a courageous one. Those who embrace this prophetic task must be ready to accept the scorn or consequences that may follow. Some might wonder how speaking truth to power aligns with the biblical call to offer a gentle answer. Christlike gentleness and prophetic strength do not cancel each other out; rather, they complete each other. It is Jesus' love—his gentleness and grace toward us—that equips us and compels us to stand up and speak out against injustice and hurt in the world. "Blessed be the God and Father of our Lord Jesus Christ, the Father of mercies and God of all comfort, who comforts us in all our affliction, so that we may be able to comfort those who are in any affliction, with the comfort with which we ourselves are comforted by God" (2 Cor. 1:3–4). Our endeavors to comfort others and fight for good will sometimes need to be expressed through bold opposition against aggressors and bullies.

German pastor, theologian, and anti-Nazi activist Dietrich Bonhoeffer paid the ultimate price for speaking in defense of Jews who were being separated from their families, imprisoned, tortured, raped, and killed through the systematic ethnic genocide that escalated during World War II. Reflecting on the risks that he and others took to ensure that the vulnerable and oppressed have a voice, Bonhoeffer wrote that Christian "discipleship means allegiance to the suffering of Christ, and it is therefore not at all surprising that Christians should be called upon to suffer. In fact, it is a joy and token of his grace."[9]

In a world in which people of faith are made especially susceptible to attack, it is imperative to recognize the vast difference between the Western, American vision and the Christian vision for happiness, health, faithfulness, and flourishing. The call of every Christian, whatever our situation, is not to overlook the horrific plight of our neighbors and our sisters and our brothers, take up our comforts, and follow our dreams—but rather to deny ourselves, take up our crosses, and follow Jesus. Either we must put ourselves at risk of enduring the mysterious "blessing" of being persecuted for our faith, or we must participate in courageous activism in defense of those who are persecuted. And perhaps, for some of us, walking faithfully with Jesus will lead to both.

HOW SHOULD WE EXPECT TO EXPERIENCE PERSECUTION?

Jesus normalized the experience of persecution for his followers, and he said it is something that we should expect rather than something we should avoid at all costs. It's also worth noting that others may insult or slight us for reasons having nothing to do with our faith. Because we live in a broken world where relational tensions abound over all sorts of things, we should expect interpersonal challenges to be part of the picture. Likewise, it is possible to stir up dissension and pushback when we *aren't* acting in line with the righteousness of Christ, but are instead acting like "jerks for Jesus." Being persecuted is *not* the same as being criticized, disliked, or overlooked because of our own judgmental and offensive postures toward our nonbelieving neighbors and the world. If our messaging and not our message is causing turmoil, we need to examine ourselves and question whether our ethics and demeanor line up with our faith.

One famously disheartening example of such misbehavior occurred after the September 11, 2001, terrorist attacks on the United States. Thousands of people died as airplanes hijacked by Islamic extremists slammed into the twin towers at the

World Trade Center in New York City and the Pentagon near Washington, DC. Another hijacked airplane crashed in a field in Pennsylvania killing all on board. Reflecting on the attack, a well-known Christian minister went on national television to offer his perspective on this unprecedented tragedy. He declared that the attack was, at its core, divine punishment of America because God was angry at our nation's moral condition. He said that God allowed the terrorists to succeed because we are a nation that allows things like abortion, homosexuality, secular education, judicial courts that are not governed by the Bible, the ACLU, and so on. In his remarks, he especially took shots at those whom he referred to as "the gays and the lesbians who are actively trying to make that an alternative lifestyle."

It did not take long for almost every kind of person, whether gay or straight, religious or nonreligious, liberal or conservative, non-Christian or Christian, to denounce this minister's public remarks.

For many of us who are Christian, the minister's remarks were disappointing—instead of passing judgment, he could have used his voice to build bridges and offer words of comfort toward a nation that was deeply hurting. Instead, he assigned blame and condemnation to certain groups. This blindness to pain and public finger-pointing is not the way of Jesus. Rather than acting in accord with Christian truth, the minister was acting squarely *out of accord* with Christian truth.

The persecution about which Jesus spoke, and which all Christians everywhere should be prepared to endure, is the kind that happens because we have been loyal to Jesus, his truth, his grace, his love, and his mission. "Blessed are you when others revile you and persecute you and utter all kinds of evil against you falsely *on my account*," Jesus said (Matt. 5:11, emphasis mine). We're talking about the kind of hostility, opposition, mistreatment, and rejection that people of faith experience because of their friendship with Jesus.

"In this world you will have trouble," Jesus said (John 16:33 NIV). "Indeed, all who desire to live a godly life in Christ Jesus will be persecuted" (2 Tim. 3:12), and "For it has been granted to you that for the sake of Christ you should not only believe in him but also suffer for his sake, engaged in the same conflict that you saw I had and now hear that I still have," wrote the apostle Paul (Phil. 1:29–30).

For those of us who identify as friends of Jesus, we must expect persecution, rejoice in persecution, live in hope when we experience persecution, and love our enemies.

Expect Persecution

Right before Jesus promised that we would experience persecution, he said, "Blessed are the peacemakers, for they shall be called sons of God" (Matt. 5:9). There is a mysterious paradox at play here. By putting "Blessed are the peacemakers" and "Blessed are those who are persecuted" together in the same teaching, Jesus is telling us that the two are not mutually exclusive. Even the greatest efforts at making peace—which, defined biblically, includes fighting for a world in which all forms of human life can flourish—can lead to opposition.

Ann Voskamp is a well-known and highly esteemed Christian writer. Ann is also known for using her platform to speak truth to power in defense of weak, vulnerable, and oppressed persons. She is what some would call a *comprehensively* pro-life activist and advocate who champions the cause of the vulnerable unborn as well as the vulnerable born—"from womb to tomb." Her message is one of compassion and advocacy for anyone under the threat of tyranny and violence at any stage of life.

In one instance, Ann used her writing platform to confront the practices of an organization widely known for its support of a woman's legal right to terminate her pregnancy, thereby also terminating the life that is developing inside of her. In another instance, she used the same writing platform to challenge those in power who seem ambivalent toward the plight of immigrants and refugees, during a time when some sixteen million souls had been exiled from their homes and communities.

As is almost always the case when someone speaks up against injustice, Ann received her (not so) fair share of criticism—from those to the political and social right as well as to the left. People from the right took issue with her stance regarding immigrants and refugees. People from the left took issue with her stance regarding the unborn. In the midst of it all, Ann faithfully committed to advocate comprehensively and not selectively for gentle treatment and rigorous advocacy on behalf of *all* vulnerable persons in the name of Christ. It became clear to Ann, as it will for every Christian openly committed to mercy and justice for all, that she was too conservative for her liberal readers and too liberal for her conservative readers. She discovered that when you seek to become God's person wholeheartedly, you also become your own person instead of merely echoing one side or another. This will inevitably draw criticism, rancor, and even disdain from both sides of the ideological and/or sociopolitical continuum.

Another example of faithfulness in the midst of opposition is the former US Surgeon General and pediatric surgeon, Dr. C. Everett Koop. After being nominated to the surgeon general's post by President Ronald Reagan in 1981, Koop had a difficult time getting through his confirmation hearings because of fierce opposition from the political left. Their chief objection to Koop was his unapologetic and public stance for the sanctity of all human life. Koop, a committed believer in Christ, had previously cowritten a book with Christian pastor and philosopher Francis Schaeffer in defense of the unborn as well as the elderly, people with disabilities and special needs, and other human souls who were being neglected and/or targeted for extinction. In this book, the two men spoke out, chiefly using scripture and human rights declarations as their basis for why they believed abortion on demand was not only bad for society, but evil. In other words, they reasoned that if all persons are created equal and possess an unalienable right to live, then all lives should be protected and cherished.

Eventually, and in spite of fierce opposition from the political left, Koop was confirmed as surgeon general. Later, however, he would come to realize that opposition during his confirmation hearings was only the beginning. But this time the opposition would not come from his opponents on the political left. Instead, it would come from his own party on the political right.

During Koop's tenure, there emerged a growing concern about a newly discovered virus, which at the time was believed to impact chiefly, if not exclusively, gay men who were sexually active. The AIDS virus, or HIV, was first discovered in 1983 and began to wreak havoc and death in epic proportions. According to an article in the *New York Times*, by 1987 some 100 million people were vulnerable to the disease and could potentially be dead by the end of the century if a cure was not discovered.[10]

In a speech at the same university founded by the minister

who would declare that the 9/11 attack was God's judgment on America, Koop expressed disappointment in his fellow conservatives—especially some of his fellow Christians—for criticizing his efforts as surgeon general to prevent the spread of HIV by providing sex education for children, as well as by informing the general public that sexual abstinence and condoms were the most effective ways to prevent the disease from advancing. "One of the things that disturbed me most," Koop reflected, "is that my own constituency, namely those political conservatives and my own religious constituents, namely evangelicals, were most critical of what I said."[11]

The stories of Ann Voskamp and C. Everett Koop illuminate what Jesus promised would happen to those who seek to follow the whole Scripture, the whole Jesus, the whole time. People who disagree from both the right and the left may oppose and reject not only your biblically formed ideas, but also you.

For those of us who are easily alarmed, hurt, or offended when others criticize us for our biblical convictions and beliefs, it is helpful to remember something else that Jesus said: "Do not think that I have come to bring peace to the earth. I have not come to bring peace, but a sword. For I have come to set a man against his father, and a daughter against her mother . . . And a person's enemies will be those of his own household . . . whoever does not take his cross and follow me is not worthy of me . . . and whoever loses his life for my sake will find it" (Matt. 10:34–39).

"The world will be offended at [Christians] and so the disciples will be persecuted for righteousness' sake," Bonhoeffer wrote. "Not recognition, but rejection, is the reward they get from their message and works."[12]

If being opposed, criticized, or mistreated because of our

"message and works" is foreign to our experience as Christians, it is wise to ask ourselves who (or what) is truly shaping and discipling us. What grips us, and what do we hold out as hope to others? Is it a political party? Is it a cable news channel? Is it a desire for public stature and reputation? Is it fear of rejection, loss of friendship, or loss of a job? Is it a friend group or an ideological echo chamber? Is it the shifting values, ethics, and dogma of the culture in which we live? Or are we being discipled, in the totality of our views, by Scripture and Jesus Christ alone?

If we identify as Christian but experience little criticism or opposition for our faith, a gut check is likely in order. Are we going along to get along? Somewhere along the way, we may have wrongly mistaken "being nice"—a popular strategy for avoiding social awkwardness or rejection—for the biblical fruit of gentleness. But as Anglican minister and writer John Stott has said, "We shouldn't be surprised [and concerned] if anti-Christian hostility increases, but rather be surprised [and concerned] if it does not."[13]

Rejoice in Persecution

Before D. Martyn Lloyd-Jones became a pastor, he was a highly esteemed, elite physician. His first ministry assignment was to a church in a blue-collar fishing town on the shores of Wales. In taking this assignment, Lloyd-Jones took a 90 percent salary reduction. What's more, the high-society elites and social circles he had once been part of smugly wrote him off for what they thought was career suicide. As they saw it, religious fanaticism had gotten the best of the esteemed doctor. Therefore, he was no longer worthy of their company.

What would compel a man to give up so much for the cause of the gospel? Some years later, Lloyd-Jones answered that question in an interview, saying, "I gave up nothing; I received everything. I count it the highest honor that God can confer on any man to call him to be a herald of the gospel."[14]

When we become less tethered to this world because we have become more tethered to Jesus Christ and the world to come, we can be certain that, ultimately, we are giving up nothing and will receive everything. As Jesus said to Peter in response to Peter's observation the disciples had left even their homes to follow him, "Truly, I say to you, there is no one who has left house or wife or brothers or parents or children, for the sake of the kingdom of God, who will not receive many times more in this time, and in the age to come eternal life" (Luke 18:28–30). In comparison to what is coming, what is lost is not to be counted. To be rejected in the eyes of the world for the sake of Christ is to be esteemed in the eyes of God. Even if the world treats us as nobodies because of our friendship with Christ, we can be certain that we've been warmly welcomed by and embraced into an eternally rejoicing and replenishing society, which is far greater than any other society this world may offer. We will be received into heaven's hall of fame and inducted into a "great cloud of witnesses," in the words of Hebrews 12, that includes the likes of Abraham, Sarah, Jacob, Hannah, Moses, Esther, Isaiah, Deborah, Jeremiah, David, Mary, Peter, James, and Paul. We will be fully joining the very family of God.

In addition to being included in God's esteemed, eternal society of saints, we can also be certain that as others oppose and reject us, we can also enjoy the privilege of what Paul called "the fellowship of sharing in [Jesus'] sufferings" (Phil. 3:10–11 NKJV). When we suffer because of our faithfulness to the grace, truth, and mission of Jesus Christ, we receive the gift of companionship with our Maker and King himself. To a persecuted church, the writer of Hebrews wrote of Jesus, "For we do not have a high priest who is unable to sympathize with our weaknesses, but one who in every respect has been tempted as we are, yet without sin. Let us then with confidence draw near to the throne of grace, that we may receive mercy and find grace to help in time of need" (4:15–16). In addition to the gift of intimacy with Christ, we also join the fellowship of those who have gone before us who have been misunderstood and mistreated because of their alignment to the Lord. "Rejoice and be glad . . . for so they persecuted the prophets who were before you" (Matt. 5:12). As John Stott said, such persecution is a token of genuineness and a certificate of Christian authenticity.[15]

Live in Hope

As we consider these difficult truths, it is important to remember the reason *why* Jesus assumes we will be able to endure opposition and injury. The reason he gives us is "for great is your reward in heaven." There is a future toward which Jesus directs his persecuted faithful. It is a future that, when grasped even partially, can unlock for us the same resources that were availed to the apostles as they faithfully endured weaknesses, insults, hardships, and intense persecution.

In *The Great Divorce*, C. S. Lewis reflected on how the future that Christ promised to us serves as our basis and resource for sharing in the fellowship of Christ's sufferings today. "Heaven, once attained," he says, "will work backwards and turn even that agony into a glory."[16]

Here, Lewis compares Christians' future to waking up from a nightmare. Whatever we lost or whatever tragic thing happened in a bad dream, waking up and realizing that the dream is no longer true makes whatever we've regained by waking up to a new day that much more precious to us. If I dream that a loved one has died, for example, and then wake up to realize she is in the kitchen eating breakfast and reading a magazine, I will walk up to her and hold her with a tighter, lengthier embrace than I would have otherwise.

In the same way, in the new heaven and new earth, each one of us will "wake up" with relief and rejoicing to a new day—a day in which there will be no more death, mourning, crying, or pain. For the old order of things will have passed away (along with opposition, violence, and persecution), and everything made new (Rev. 21:1–8). In a mysterious way, our enjoyment of heaven will be that much sweeter to us, not in spite of the fact that we suffered, but *because* of the fact that we suffered. We will wake up from the nightmare into an everlasting, glorious new day.

LOVE YOUR ENEMIES, JUST AS YOU HAVE BEEN LOVED

This future hope to which Jesus directs us is just one of the reasons why we can endure hardship, criticism, and persecution. In addition to urging us to look ahead to the world that is to come, he also urges us to look back to the way he loved us and gave himself for us: "God shows his love for us in that while we were *still sinners*, Christ died for us" (Rom. 5:8, emphasis mine).

While we were still sinners. While we were still opposed to him. While we were turning our backs on him. While we were mocking and maligning and mischaracterizing him. While we were persecuting him and blaming him and uttering all kinds of evil against him. *That* is precisely when Christ died for us.

Understanding the lengths to which Jesus went to reconcile himself to us can powerfully motivate us to endure opposition *and* respond to our opponents not with defensiveness and retaliatory anger, but instead with love. For the gentle answer of Jesus toward our violent and oppressive ways has turned *our* wrath away, and has drawn us in to love him, just as he has loved us.

In the biographical film *Schindler's List*, Oscar Schindler, nemesis to Nazis and protector of Jewish refugees, says, "Power . . . is when we have every justification to kill, and we don't."[17] This was precisely the stance that Jesus Christ assumed when he gave his life for us on the cross. Because we sinned against him, because we perpetrated violence and injury to both his Name and his Person, Jesus had every justification to kill us . . . and he didn't.

It is because we have been treated with such kindness, such grace, such gentleness that we ought to be the most difficult people in the world to offend. Christ chose to turn *God's* justifiable wrath away from *us* by absorbing that very wrath himself through substitution, sacrifice, and forgiveness. His is a radical forgiveness that was bought with persecution, blood, and martyrdom. It is Christ's unmerited love for us that serves as the basis for not only becoming the best kinds of friends, but also the best kinds of enemies that the world will ever know.

AN OLD DOG *CAN* LEARN NEW TRICKS

The Christian minister I mentioned earlier in this chapter—the one who said regrettable things about the September 11 terrorist attacks—would apologize for his remarks three days after making them. The minister was Rev. Jerry Falwell, also the chief figurehead of the political movement known as the Moral Majority. In a phone call to CNN, he said, "I would never blame any human being except the terrorists, and if I left that impression with gays or lesbians or anyone else, I apologize."[18]

Another person who experienced public criticism from Falwell was Larry Flynt, founder and publisher of *Hustler*, a pornographic magazine known for its disturbingly graphic images of naked women. Beginning in the early 1970s, a public war of words ensued between the two men. According to Flynt, "Falwell was blasting me every chance he had. He would talk about how I was a slime dealer responsible for the decay of all morals. He called me every terrible name he could think of—names as bad, in my opinion, as any language used in my magazine."[19]

After several years trading insults with each other, Flynt ran an ad in *Hustler* mocking Falwell and parodying the minister describing his first time having sexual intercourse. In the parody, the made-up version of Falwell lost his virginity with his mother while both were drunk and in an outhouse.

Feeling hurt and smeared by the parody, Falwell filed a libel suit against Flynt in federal court, beginning a five-year battle that went all the way to the Supreme Court. To both men's surprise, Flynt and *Hustler* won the case. Offended by the outcome, Falwell publicly criticized the decision and referred to Flynt as a "sleaze merchant."

But ten years later, the relationship between the minister and the pornographer took a different turn. Being high-profile, public enemies made them perfect ratings material for talk shows, and the two men were invited to continue sparring with one another in front of eight million viewers on *Larry King Live*. According to Flynt, this was the first time he and Falwell had been in the same room together since the Supreme Court decision. The fact that he and the minister were breathing the same air was enough to make him feel sick.

At one point during the interview, Falwell did what no one—especially Flynt—expected him to do. Instead of calling names and expressing outrage and adding to an already well-developed list of insults, Jerry Falwell reached over and gave Larry Flynt a warm, affectionate hug.

Initially and understandably, Flynt was very confused by Falwell's gesture. And then, a few days later, the minister showed up unannounced at the *Hustler* office. Flynt's assistant summoned him, announcing, "Jerry Falwell is here to see you." Surprised, Flynt nonetheless told her to send him in. With a stack of *Hustler* magazines in between them, the two talked for several hours. There and then, the two agreed to travel the country together, discussing and debating their divergent ideas on college campuses.

According to Flynt, in the years that followed their tour of the country and leading up to Falwell's death, Falwell would come visit Flynt every time he was in Flynt's home state of California. During these visits, they would continue their respectful conversations and debate around their most deeply held—and radically different—ideas. They got to know one another's families, exchanged cards and gifts during the holidays, and supported one another in their shared struggles related to health and aging.

After Falwell's death in 2007, in a eulogy published in the *Los Angeles Times* entitled "My Friend, Jerry Falwell," Flynt said the following:

> The truth is, the reverend and I had a lot in common . . . We steered our conversations away from politics, but religion was within bounds. He wanted to save me and was determined to get me out of "the business."
>
> My mother always told me that no matter how repugnant you find a person, when you meet them face to face you will always find something about them to like. The more I got to know Falwell, the more I began to see that his public portrayals were caricatures . . . in the end, I knew what he was selling, and he knew what I was selling, and we found a way to communicate.
>
> Every time I'd call him, I'd get put right through, and he'd let me berate him about his views . . . I'm sure I never changed his mind about anything, just as he never changed mine. I'll never admire him for his views or his opinions . . . but the ultimate result was one I never expected and was just as shocking a turn to me as was winning that famous Supreme Court case: We became friends.

Perhaps this is the sort of thing Jesus envisioned when he said that we should love not only our friends who think and believe as we do, but also (and especially) our enemies who don't. Perhaps this is the sort of thing he envisioned when he said we should pray for those who persecute us and say all kinds of false, unflattering, and hurtful things about us.

For if Christians don't *go first* in offering a gentle answer to those who oppose us, can we ever expect those who oppose us to make a similar move? And if Christians don't take the first step to humble ourselves and become less testy, less defensive, less easily offended, and less vindictive when we experience milder forms of opposition and criticism than the global norm, who will?

QUESTIONS FOR REFLECTION AND DISCUSSION

1. Name one thing from this chapter that troubled you, inspired you, or both. Why were you impacted in this way?
2. Have you ever experienced persecution? If so, describe the experience. How did it impact your relationship with Christ? With other people?
3. In what ways has the American Dream shaped your expectations of how Christians are treated by society? In what ways have American politics shaped your expectations?
4. Based on this chapter, identify one way that the Lord might be nudging you toward growth or change. What steps should you take to pursue the change?

FIVE

We Do Anger Well

As someone once said, "Anger is an acid that can do more harm to the vessel in which it is stored than to anything onto which it is poured." Similarly, Anne Lamott has said that nursing a grudge against someone is like drinking rat poison and then waiting for the rat to die.[1] These sayings are getting at essentially the same thing. Anger, when released from its cage and allowed to run wild, backfires and devours the angry person's soul.

I have been hurt deeply by others. Have you? Whether we've been betrayed, stolen from, lied to, gossiped about, slandered, or bullied, sometimes it feels natural to cling to anger, to wish ill upon the offending party, and to start fighting fire with fire. It is easy to excuse and exempt ourselves from the biblical command to forgive as God in Christ has forgiven us, let alone to respond with a gentle answer. When anger gets the best of us, we can resort to replacing grace with grudges. We can talk ourselves into believing that if we stay angry toward those who have harmed us, we can keep power over them. However, nursing a grudge accomplishes the opposite. Nursing a grudge actually gives those who have harmed us an invitation to continue having power over us. As Frederick Buechner observed, "To lick your wounds, to smack your lips over grievances long past, to roll over your tongue the prospect of bitter confrontations still to come, to savor to the last toothsome morsel both the pain you are given and the pain you are giving back—in many ways it is a feast fit for a king. The chief drawback is that what you are wolfing down is yourself. The skeleton at the feast is you."[2]

Initially, resentment tastes delicious to us. But the deliciousness is only momentary. It's only a matter of time before it starts working against us. To survive, we must find a way to expel the toxins of destructive anger.

On the flip side, there is a certain kind of anger that scripture not only allows, but commands. Once in the Psalms and once in Paul's letter to the Ephesians, we are told that when anger is justified, we should "be angry, and do not sin" (Ps. 4:4; Ephesians 4:26 NKJV). Some Christians may have difficulty with this kind of language. On the surface it sounds contradictory to the Sermon on the Mount, where Jesus told us to turn the other cheek when someone strikes us and to love our enemies and bless and pray for those who persecute us.

Similarly, some may object to biblical teachings about God judging and punishing his enemies. In other words, there are times when God gets angry with those who oppose him and his ways. In scripture, God is referred to as a consuming fire whose wrath is revealed against all the ungodliness and unrighteousness of men, who by their unrighteousness suppress the truth (Rom. 1:18; Heb. 12:29). When the reality of God's anger and judgment is highlighted, some object strongly. "This is why I don't like the Bible and Christianity. If there is a god at all for me, it's not an angry god. My god is loving! My god would never lash out or punish or judge or get angry at people!"

When I hear someone discount or downplay the biblical idea of God as a judge whose holiness sometimes includes expressions of anger, I wonder if they've ever been the bullied kid, or the abused woman, or the oppressed slave, or the assaulted victim. I wonder if they've ever sat down and listened to the story of a Holocaust victim, or of someone whose child was kidnapped, or of a woman whose husband abandoned her for a younger mistress. When one has experienced deep injustice, one yearns desperately for someone to take action and make things right and whole once again. To suggest that God is a loving God who can never be angry is to promote falsehood. To suggest that Christ's call to turn the other cheek and love our enemies is incompatible with anger is not only false, but potentially damaging, especially to injured parties.

Several years ago, I came across an article about a pamphlet distributed by an elementary school to its students. The pamphlet offered advice to children who were bullied by their peers. Whenever they were insulted, made fun of, or injured by another student, those on the receiving end were to respond according to the following nine rules:

Rule #1: Refuse to get mad.
Rule #2: Treat the person who is being mean as if they are trying to help you.
Rule #3: Do not be afraid.
Rule #4: Do not verbally defend yourself.
Rule #5: Do not attack.

Rule #6: If someone physically hurts you . . . do not get angry.

Rule #7: Do not tell on bullies.

Rule #8: Don't be a sore loser.

Rule #9: Learn to laugh at yourself and not get "hooked by put-downs."[3]

Appropriately, the title of the article was, "US School Provides Worst Bullying Advice Ever." It seems to me that the list could have been written by the bullies themselves. Rather than providing a solution to hurtful behavior, the rules set forth in the pamphlet only embolden the bullies and perpetuate the bullying. Indeed, this advice was the *worst* advice ever.

RIGHTEOUS ANGER THAT FIGHTS FOR *SHALOM*

During the civil rights era, Dr. Martin Luther King Jr. and the millions of other people of color residing in the United States had plenty of reasons to be upset. Their history and personal experience included evils committed against them—such as slavery, Jim Crow laws, economic inequality and exploitation, segregation, denial of access to restaurants, hotels, public restrooms, and transportation, and being terrorized by white supremacists and the Ku Klux Klan and even, at times, the police.

In his heartfelt *Letter from a Birmingham Jail*, King expressed his deep disappointment toward white ministers who privately assured him that they were on his side and cheering for his cause, while at the same time refusing to go public with their support.

Likewise, his anger over the injustice of things can be felt in this sobering statement, written on behalf of all people of color:

> Perhaps it is easy for those who have never felt the stinging darts of segregation to say, "Wait." But when you have seen vicious mobs lynch your mothers and fathers at will and drown your sisters and brothers at whim; when you have seen hate filled policemen curse, kick and even kill your black brothers and sisters; when you see the vast majority of your twenty million Negro brothers smothering in an airtight cage of poverty in the midst of an affluent society; when you suddenly find your tongue twisted and your speech stammering as you seek to explain to your six year old daughter why she can't go to the public amusement park that has just been advertised on television, and see tears welling up in her eyes when she is told that Funtown is closed to colored children, and see ominous clouds of inferiority beginning to form in her little mental sky, and see her beginning to distort her personality by developing an unconscious bitterness toward white people; when you have to concoct an answer for a five year old son who is asking: "Daddy, why do white people treat colored people so mean?"; when you take a cross county drive and find it necessary to sleep night after night in the uncomfortable corners of your automobile because no motel will accept you; when you are humiliated day in and day out by nagging signs reading "white" and "colored"; when your first name becomes "nigger," your middle name becomes "boy" (however old you are) and your last name becomes "John," and your wife and mother are never given the respected title "Mrs."; when you are harried by day and haunted by night by the fact that you are a Negro,

> living constantly at tiptoe stance, never quite knowing what to expect next, and are plagued with inner fears and outer resentments; when you are forever fighting a degenerating sense of "nobodiness"—then you will understand why we find it difficult to wait. There comes a time when the cup of endurance runs over, and men are no longer willing to be plunged into the abyss of despair. I hope, sirs, you can understand our legitimate and unavoidable impatience.[4]

According to King, people of color were left fending for themselves in a world that was stacked against them. With little patience left for such neglect and betrayal, he wrote, "We know through painful experience that freedom is never voluntarily given by the oppressor; it must be demanded by the oppressed."[5]

King did make demands, which eventually caused white leaders, including President Lyndon B. Johnson, to begin taking the cause of racial equality and justice seriously. Though we still have a long way to go, no one would argue that King's contribution—much of which was borne from what we call *righteous* anger—moved the ball forward significantly in the realm of civil rights. In addition to his courageous leadership, King also modeled a specific *way* of expressing anger that embodied and promoted righteousness as opposed to sin. In his 1964 Nobel Peace Prize acceptance speech, King described his method as follows:

> This award which I receive on behalf of a movement is a profound recognition that *nonviolence* is the answer to the critical political and moral question of our time—the need for man to overcome oppression and violence without resorting to

> violence and oppression . . . Man must evolve for all human conflict a method which rejects revenge, aggression, and retaliation. The foundation for such a method is love.[6]

Another example is the well-known Catholic nun who lived most of her life in Calcutta, India. Mother Teresa served thousands of desperately poor, sick, and forgotten people. In 1994 she was invited to the United States by the proudly pro-choice President Bill Clinton to give the keynote speech at the National Prayer Breakfast. In that speech, she channeled her own God-given anger by boldly and courageously speaking against the termination of image-bearing children in the womb.

Barely visible from behind the podium due to her small stature, she said, "If we accept that a mother can kill even her own child, how can we tell other people not to kill one another? [Abortion] just leads to more abortion. Any country that accepts abortion is not teaching its people to love one another but to use any violence to get what they want."[7]

The prophetic nun then looked toward the president at the head table and pleaded with him to stop terminating children in the womb and give them to her instead. As many in the crowd erupted in applause, the president, vice president, and their wives sat uncomfortably at the head table. One religious leader remarked afterward that Mother Teresa's words were "as bold a prophetic confrontation as [we've] ever witnessed."[8]

Mother Teresa's courageous commitment to use negative emotion—whether it was sorrow, grief, anger, or some combination thereof—for good by speaking truth to power is an example of how we must be willing, even if it costs us, to *stand* on behalf of all who are weak, vulnerable, or unjustly persecuted. Without resorting to vindictiveness or violence or retribution, we must be willing not only to feel, but to voice the anger of God against all forms of unjust violence toward human bodies and souls. Christianity—far from being a disinterested, passive religion with respect to the violation of human rights—must go on the offense. As C. S. Lewis reminds us, "Christianity is a fighting religion . . . [that thinks] that a great many things have gone wrong with the world that God made and that God insists, and insists very loudly, on our putting them right again."[9]

In our current culture of outrage and us-against-them, what does it mean for us to be angry *and* sin not? We can take a deeper look at this concept of fighting in a way that doesn't compromise or negate the fruit of gentleness, but rather upholds it.

ANGER THAT IS GOOD

Anger is a powerful energy that, in the hands of a Spirit-filled person or group, can be channeled in constructive and life-giving ways. Indeed, all forms of anger are not equal, and not all forms of anger are wrong. According to the Bible, it is possible to be angry *and* loving, furious *and* full of grace . . . all at the same time. This healthy kind of anger that the Bible commends is motivated by love.

There are toxic forms of anger, and there are also healthy ones. As opposed to stealing and diminishing life like poison or a wildfire, healthy anger produces life-giving outcomes. Compelled by love, healthy anger resembles the Spirit's fruit of *patience*. It resists the impulse to strike back or seek revenge. It leaves both the discernment and execution of ultimate justice in God's hands.

And yet, where possible, healthy anger can also be harnessed to destroy. While toxic anger destroys the good in order to promote evil, healthy anger seeks to destroy evil in order to promote and protect the good. *Be angry, and do not sin.*

Jesus Wasn't Nice

Many of us were told in childhood, "If you don't have something nice to say, don't say anything at all!" This kind of thinking is understandable because most of us would rather be around a nice person than an angry person. Nice people are pleasant and unobtrusive. They rarely stir the pot, are easy to please, and are low maintenance. But nice people aren't always healthy people. Nice people, in their reluctance to confront, can sometimes work against the purposes of God.

Jesus wasn't always nice.

Sometimes Jesus was the furthest thing from nice.

Jesus is humble, gentle, and kind. As scripture assures us, his yoke is easy and his burden is light. He invites the weary and burdened to come to him for support and comfort (Matt. 11:28–32). Yet Jesus is also a consuming fire who sets us straight when we are out of line. Sometimes Jesus puts us in our place—not in spite of the fact that he loves us, but *because* he loves us. *Jesus got angry.*

Appalled by corrupt worship practices and attitudes, Jesus flipped over tables in the temple (Matt. 21:12–13). The Son of God had what looked like a tantrum—in church. Can you imagine? He called people names like *hypocrites* and *whitewashed tombs* and *children of the devil*—especially when they used religion to bully, control, and abuse people (Matt. 23:13–39). When Peter, one of his closest friends, tempted him to pursue comfort over faithfulness and power over self-sacrifice, Jesus got so worked up that he called Peter "Satan" (Matt. 16:23). Peering into the tomb of his friend Lazarus, Jesus got madder than a rodeo bull. Death, the wages of sin and the last enemy of those who have been redeemed from sin, infuriated Jesus (John 11:17–44). When Jesus returns again to make all things new, he will bring his recompense with him, to repay Satan and bullies and perpetrators of injustice for their evil (Rev. 22:12). In these and other instances, Jesus shows that it is possible, even Godlike, for him to get steaming mad. He shows that it is possible to lose our cool without losing our character. Sometimes anger, when released from a place of health and love, is a furious force that accomplishes constructive and life-giving outcomes.

Love Detests Whatever Injures or Destroys

When the apostle Paul wrote, "Hate what is evil; cling to what is good" (Rom. 12:9 NIV), he was advocating for the healthy, love-driven kind of anger. Hatred toward evil, according to Paul, is a by-product of love for the good. Anger reveals the things that we love most. We only get angry when something or someone we love is threatened, oppressed, or abused. When we *love* what is good, we naturally abhor things like abuse, theft, disease, depression, and death. We hate injustice, poverty, dishonesty, and spin. We hate seeing children neglected, spouses abandoned, the elderly and poor forgotten. We hate these things, and we get *angry* about them because we feel protective of the excellent, pure, lovely, and praiseworthy things they threaten and contradict. It's a holy kind of anger. It's anger compelled by *shalom*, the wise and healthy vision for the world as God intended it to be, for God's kingdom to come on earth as it is in heaven. It is the kind of anger that says, "I want more. I want better. I want health, life, goodness, protection, truth, and beauty for the people, places, and things God loves . . . for every soul and square inch that God intends to redeem." It's the kind of anger that protects the most vulnerable from violence and injury, and preserves for them the assurance that their wounds will be treated with gentleness and care.

Author Rebecca Pippert said that true love detests whatever injures or destroys those we love. True love will protest against whatever threatens to bring harm to our beloved. If a little girl disobeys her mother's instruction to stay away from moving cars and instead chooses to run into a busy street, the mother will scream and attempt to stop her behavior. The mother will express anger—not because she doesn't love her daughter but because she does love her dearly. It is the language of loving concern, aimed at protecting her from her own foolishness and self-destructive behavior. Likewise, if a young man is destroying himself through substance abuse, his father will despise the alcohol or the drugs that have him around the neck. The father will do everything within his power to fight against his son's self-destructive choices and behaviors—not because he is opposed to his son, but because he is *for* his son's sobriety and health. "The more a father loves his son," Pippert wrote, "the more he hates in him the drunkard, the liar, the traitor . . . Anger isn't the opposite of love. Hate is, and the final form of hate is indifference."[10]

Sometimes anger can be the highest compliment and the deepest assurance that someone cares for us. This is true especially when the anger directed toward us comes from someone who aims to protect us and make us into the most life-giving versions of ourselves.

Do we assume that Christians are supposed to approach conflict by merely speaking and acting politely? Do we think it's godly to just "play nice"? If so, we've got to come to understand that Scripture does not support this position. While the Bible does urge us to be patient, gracious, and kind toward others just as God is toward us, it does not insist that we always be nice. The Old Testament is full of God-inspired prayers by real people, many of whom were under great pressure and were being persecuted and injured. Their prayers, far from being nice, were filled with words of righteous, divinely sanctioned anger followed by prayers of thanksgiving to a God who will deliver his people from their enemies.

Anger in Our Prayers

"May the Lord see and avenge," prays Joash, the Israelite king (2 Chron. 24:22). "Lord . . . take vengeance for me on my persecutors" (Jer. 15:15); and "Bring on them the day of disaster; destroy them with double destruction" (17:18 niv); and "Let me see your vengeance upon them" (11:20), prays the prophet Jeremiah. "Deal with them in anger," says the prophet Ezekiel (8:18 niv). And then there are all those imprecatory psalms, prayers inspired by God for the people of God, that call down judgment on God's enemies as well as theirs (e.g., Pss. 5, 10, 17, 35, 58, 59, 69, 70, 79, 83, 109, 129, 137, and 140).

The expressions of anger contained in these biblical prayers give vent and voice to pain. God knows we need a safe and nondestructive outlet to let out all the hurt we feel. He gives us an emotion like anger as a vehicle of protest in a world that has gone wrong. Shouting our pain to God is one of the most reverent things we can do. It reveals that we recognize a God who is there, a God who cares, a God who can take action on our behalf. Venting reveals hope, yet it is also important that we vent our anger first to God. Only then will we gain the proper perspective on how to take the same anger to those who are the source of it. Rather than striking back to even the score, the spiritual person prays his or her hurt and angry feelings directly to God.

It is possible to be angry without committing sin. In certain instances, it would actually be a sin to withhold or stuff down anger. We are to simultaneously hate what is evil and cling to what is good (Rom. 12:9). And the more we learn about Jesus and become like him, the more we understand that clinging to what is good often requires us to hate what is evil, because evil is the enemy of good.

When Jesus expresses anger, it is always with a view toward defending and protecting something good or someone he loves. Perhaps this is why he refers to himself as a physician. "Those who are well have no need of a physician, but those who are sick," Jesus said (Mark 2:17). Part of what it means to be a *good* physician is to be angry at and opposed to injuries, bacteria, viruses, cancers, and other invasive realities that threaten health. As the ultimate good physician, Jesus harnessed righteous anger and resolved to fight the most invasive threat to human flourishing—the reality of sin itself.

ANGER THAT IS LIFE-DIMINISHING

While there is a form of anger that is life-giving, there is also a more common form that is life-diminishing. This is the kind of anger spoken of in the proverb that says, "A fool gives full vent to his spirit, but a wise man quietly holds it back" (Prov. 29:11). Similarly, Ecclesiastes warns, "Be not quick in your spirit to become angry, for anger lodges in the heart of fools" (Eccl. 7:9). This is not the life-giving, love-motivated anger that God commands and supports. On the contrary, life-diminishing anger is motivated by resentment, retaliation, and an intent to destroy. It's the kind of anger that leads to murderous sins of heart and tongue such as wrath, malice, slander, obscene talk, manipulation, control, and hatred. It's the kind of anger about which Jesus spoke when he said, "I say to you that everyone who is angry with his brother will be liable to judgment; whoever insults his brother will be liable to the council; and whoever says, 'You fool!' will be liable to the hell of fire" (Matt. 5:22). This is toxic anger.

When Anger Turns Toxic

Toxic anger works against *shalom*. Instead of promoting life as healthy anger does, toxic anger destroys and diminishes life. It is not restorative; it is retaliatory and punitive, vengeful and aggressive, unrestrained and uncontained. Toxic anger doesn't leave things better. It makes things worse.

Anger can be compared to fire. Fire, like anger, has a lot of redeeming uses. It protects and warms us in the colder months, creates lovely ambience with a fireplace or a candle, and kills the destructive bacteria residing in our food. But if we don't keep fire inside boundaries, if we let it run wild, then it has the potential to destroy an entire house, or a forest, or human life. Let fire rage and it will steal, kill, and destroy whatever and whomever lies in its path.

How do we hold and express anger inside healthy boundaries? How do we use it to leave things better and not make things worse? What can we do to keep it from spreading like wildfire? It starts with the little things. It starts with how we handle the things that trigger us most easily. As Jesus said, "One who is faithful in a very little is also faithful in much" (Luke 16:10).

Redeeming Our Pet (and Petty) Peeves

I have two pet peeves that can lead me into unrighteous anger. One of these is my impatience in traffic. When a car in front of me is going too slowly for my taste, I am tempted to belittle the driver in my heart. Or if another driver treats me like I am the problem because I am going too slow for their taste, I will tell myself that they must be emotionally unstable and completely unhinged.

I once heard the comedian George Carlin do a special on what causes road rage. In his remarks, he said that "anybody driving slower than you is an idiot, and anybody driving faster than you is a maniac" according to a survey about driving habits.[11] In other words, "diva" drivers like me think that there are basically three kinds of drivers. First, there are the good drivers. This group includes us and those who stay out of our way. Second, there are the idiot drivers. This group includes those who drive too slowly, take in the scenery, look both ways more than once, and stop at yellow lights. Lastly, there are the maniac drivers. This group includes those who zoom past us in the same way that we zoom past the idiot drivers. Which of course means that we, too, are the idiots and maniacs to everyone else on the road.

In addition to my driving issues, Patti and our daughters have the misfortune of living with a man (me) who gets easily irritated by eating noises. For as long as I can remember, the sound of others chewing and crunching and slurping has set me off like fingernails on a chalkboard. I recently discovered that this quirk of mine is an actual medical condition called *misophonia,* which means "the hatred of sound." Sometimes my irritation with chewing has been so annoying that family members have removed themselves from my presence so they could eat in peace.

Someone recently sent me a link to an article about misophonia, which stated that this condition is a sign of intelligence. I forwarded the link to Patti. She was not impressed. Actually, she expressed frustration at how this "pet peeve" of mine had put family members in the awkward position of walking on eggshells during meals. Patti reminded me that my misophonia is also a form of hypocrisy because I eat popcorn, chew gum, and sip coffee louder than just about anyone.

Another thing I have discovered about my misophonia—my little *pet peeve*—is that it is God's gift to me for the formation of my character. Misophonia presses me to make thousands of minidecisions to cooperate with the Holy Spirit. Instead of harboring or expressing impatient, aggressive anger when I don't like what I hear, I can yield to the Spirit's work of growing patience, gentleness, and self-control in my life. The cumulative effect of nurturing the fruit of the Spirit in these frequent, small moments enlarges my capacity for health when a bigger irritant or even a true injustice comes my way.

Because one who is faithful with little is also faithful with much.

Just as strong biceps and a healthy heart are cultivated by daily workout habits, love's virtues are cultivated through daily faithfulness in the small things. We will tell truth under pressure only when we have resisted the daily habit of exaggerating and telling white lies. We will faithfully give financially from a big salary only when we have nurtured a habit of giving the same proportion on a smaller salary. And when it comes to anger, we will become patient and full of grace in the big offenses only if we have first nurtured the daily patience and grace with smaller obstacles. If we don't nurture patience in the little things, we will struggle to forgive when the bigger hurts and betrayals come. And they *will* come.

The way to protect ourselves and others from the wildfire that sparks of anger can become is through attentive and faithful stewardship of the minor, daily irritants in our lives. As a treadmill and a set of weights in the gym serve as instruments for physical health, other things like a crying baby at 3:00 a.m., an unanticipated and costly car repair, an annoying remark on social media, or a snoring spouse can serve as instruments for our spiritual health. Each daily challenge or pet peeve presents us with an opportunity to either feed or starve our toxic anger impulse. As a safeguard from such destructive anger, we must heed what the Lord said to Cain who harbored resentment against his brother, Abel: "Sin is crouching at the door. Its desire is contrary to you, but you must rule over it" (Gen. 4:7). And as the great Puritan preacher John Owen wrote, "Be killing sin or it will be killing you."[12]

Sin with a Capital *S*

There is a lot at stake here. Anger, once it is allowed to turn toxic, can destroy your life and leave a trail of sorrow behind you. It can lead to crumbled friendships and marriages, to shooting sprees and murder, to emotional and physical abuse, and to wars. It can also lead to the assassination of someone's character through gossip, slander, and mischaracterization, as we often see in political campaigns, on social media feeds, in teen culture, and in church conflicts.

Gossip and slander, two devious fruits of toxic anger, do deep and sometimes irreversible damage to a person's good name.

Gossip can be compared to pornography in that both seek cheap thrills at another person's expense, while making zero commitment to the other person. Contrary to love, gossip objectifies and depersonifies.

Slander takes gossip to the next level. According to *Merriam-Webster, slander* is defined as the utterance of false charges or misrepresentations that defame and damage another's reputation. Old Testament scholar and Covenant Seminary professor Jay Sklar called this soul-crushing and community-killing evil exactly what it is: "To slander is to throw acid onto the face of another's reputation. It mars them in the cruelest ways . . . Slander is Sin with a capital S."[13]

WHEN INJURY AND OFFENSE RUN DEEP

Some may be thinking, "What about justice and betrayal? When deep hurts and betrayals happen to us, are we supposed to just roll over like a doormat and let people step all over us?" How do we keep anger healthy in these desperate struggles?

Did Jesus consider these questions when he said that we should forgive our enemies? Were these things on his radar when he said to bless and pray for those who persecute us and say all kinds of false things about us? Did he account for offenses against us that feel like the ripping of flesh, that feel like an assault to the soul, that feel like being crucified?

We long for someone to take what is wrong and make it right. Once you or a loved one has been gossiped about, slandered, injured, betrayed, or abused, you begin to realize how much you need—how much the whole world needs—a God who ultimately will not let people get away with hurting other people. You begin to realize how much the world needs a God who attacks evil in order to defend and protect the good, who puts his foot down with bullies and removes them from the playground, who gives perpetrators of injustice their due and comforts the victims.

Only those who know that God will set every wrong right can truly forgive as God in Christ has forgiven them. Only those who know this will have the ability to *pursue* justice but to also *entrust* justice—especially the punitive, retributive payback justice—into the hands of the One who judges justly and who alone has the power to make everything right again. It is only those who know God not only as their Father but also as their Defender who will be angry but not sin in their anger (Eph. 4:26). It is only those who know this who will be able to lose their cool—like Jesus' outburst in the temple, hating what is evil but clinging to what is good—without losing their character.

And there's one more thing God gives us to help us in our longing for justice, in our anger. There's one more thing he gives us so we will have an inner resource to bear injury without having a meltdown. What is it?

It's the same gift that Dr. Martin Luther King Jr. gave to white people who insulted him, sucker-punched him, and eventually killed him. It's the gift of nonretaliation.

God, who had every right to retaliate against *us*, to turn the tables upside down on us and put us in our place once and for all . . . chose not to. For "God demonstrates his own love for us in this: While we were still sinners, Christ died for us" (Rom. 5:8 NIV). Jesus cried out on the cross, "Father, forgive them, for they do not know what they are doing" (Luke 23:34 NIV).

Jesus gave his life for us, he prayed that we would be

forgiven—and he did so not when we were at our best, but when we were at our worst. Not when we were compassionate and gentle and kind, but when we were mean and belligerent and cruel. While we were *still* sinners—denying, insulting, ignoring, abusing, and crucifying him—that is when Christ died for us.

This is the power of a gentle answer turning away wrath. This is the power that enables us to expel the poison of toxic anger and to, instead, give expression to anger motivated and moved by love. Could there be any better reason to treasure the Spirit's powerful fruit of gentleness in our own lives?

Be angry, and sin not.

QUESTIONS FOR REFLECTION AND DISCUSSION

1. Name one thing from this chapter that troubled you, inspired you, or both. Why were you impacted in this way?
2. Is the idea of anger as a virtue and gift from God new to you? How would you describe the difference between unrighteous anger and righteous anger? Can you give an example of each, from either observation or experience?
3. We've discussed how our smaller pet peeves can become a training ground to prepare us for dealing faithfully with greater injuries and offenses. What are your pet peeves? How is your response to them preparing you for future conflicts, whether for good or for ill?
4. Based on this chapter, identify one way that the Lord might be nudging you toward growth or change. What steps should you take to pursue the change?

SIX

We Receive Criticism Graciously

I hate it when people criticize me.

Yet criticism is to be expected. Even the best parents get criticized by their children, bosses by their employees, coaches by their players, athletes by their fans, teachers by their students, artists by their critics, and pastors by their congregants.

Over the years, I think I have gotten better about receiving criticism from the people around me. When the criticism is fair, it actually helps me see my blind spots, address my weaknesses, and improve my efforts at loving and leading those around me. However, when the criticism is not fair, I sometimes react in a negative and defensive way. And, honestly, I sometimes react poorly when the criticism *is* fair.

Recently, a man who had visited our church while traveling through Nashville sent me a public criticism on Twitter, telling me all of the things that, in his "humble opinion," were wrong about my sermon. Feeling defensive and irritated, I foolishly retaliated with a criticism of my own, along with a Bible verse to justify my response. (In chapter 3, I explain why my heart can sometimes jump to defensiveness when I feel I am being wrongly criticized. Even in middle age, this remains a growth area for me.) The man then sent five more messages on Twitter, piling on more criticism and taking my words out of context. I responded a second time, again in a way that was not helpful.

My friend and longtime encourager, pastor Scotty Smith, saw the exchange between me and the church visitor. He swiftly sent me a text message that said, "Scott, my brother, you forgot that you're not supposed to wrestle with pigs."

Scotty's text was not intended as an insult to the man on Twitter. Rather, he was reminding me of a phrase that he and I had picked up from an article by leadership expert Carey Nieuwhof. "Don't wrestle with pigs" is another way of saying that when people try to pick a fight or when they seem bent on criticizing you, it's usually best simply not to engage them. Why? Because when we "wrestle with pigs," we run the risk of becoming pig-headed ourselves in the process, with everybody ending up muddy.

There is another cost to wrestling with pigs. When we harshly fight back instead of seeking to defuse a situation by responding with a gentle answer, we condition ourselves to reject all criticism, even the kind that *is* fair. When this occurs, we are listening to the twisted voice of our own self-righteousness instead of resting in the righteousness that has been given to us freely in Christ. When we wrestle with pigs, it can be to our own peril.

THE BATTLE WITHIN US

The potential for powerful good and the potential for deep evil exists in each one of us. We are, simultaneously, both Dr. Jekyll and Mr. Hyde. Scripture says of this dual reality that we are saints and sinners, old man and new man, flesh and spirit. We are, as Luther said, *simul iustus et peccator*—at the same time righteous and law-breakers. This means that we are capable of heroic love *and* horrible hatred at all times.

A few years ago, our staff at church did an exercise involving the sixteen different Myers-Briggs personality styles. This included identifying which historical figures each of us resembled most. It was discovered that as an INFJ, I share a personality profile with two very well-known people from the past: Jesus Christ and Adolf Hitler. This simultaneously encouraging and alarming observation simply confirms what the Bible tells me: inside me, simultaneously, resides both spirit and flesh, both faithfulness and sinfulness, both the capacity to love greatly and the capacity to injure severely.

Even the apostle Paul, one of the greatest Christian leaders who ever lived, recognized this duality about himself as he wrote in his letter to the Romans, "I do not understand my own actions. For I do not do what I want, but I do the very thing I hate . . . I have the desire to do what is right, but not the ability to carry it out. For I do not do the good I want, but the evil I do not want is what I keep on doing . . . when I want to do right, evil lies close at hand" (7:15–21).

Thankfully for all of us, this was not the end of the story for Paul. Having been brought low by his sin, he continued in the next chapter of Romans to provide the hope-filled solution to his and our deepest problem. There is no condemnation in Christ, who has rescued and redeemed us from the curse of God's law. Christ, who is our legal advocate before the judgment seat of God, also gives his Spirit to dwell inside of us. The Spirit helps us to pray when we don't know how, directs our minds toward the things of the Spirit and away from the things of the flesh, and reminds us that nothing in all creation will ever be able to separate us from his love (Rom. 8:1–39). To the degree that we understand and internalize these truths about our secure standing in Christ, we can experience freedom from our Jekyll and Hyde duality as Paul did. We can begin to see our sin for what it is—*absurd*—while we also get about the pursuit of help outside of ourselves, which is a help that only God can provide.

The Absurdity of Sin

God responds to our sin with reassurance instead of shame, kindness instead of punishment, mercy instead of judgment, and love instead of abandonment. This reality presses us to consider why we would ever want to continue sinning. As the late–nineteenth-century pastor C. H. Spurgeon wrote, "God is more ready to forgive than I am to offend."[1] If it is true that it is not our repentance that leads God to be kind but God's kindness that leads us to repent (Rom. 2:4), then why would we ever consider *not* repenting of our sin? If God has moved our judgment day from the future to the past through the perfect life and atoning death of Jesus, why would we ever think it right or good to continue living in ways that are worthy of judgment?

Sin is absurd and futile, especially for Christians who are aware of the love and redeeming grace of God through Jesus. It is absurd and futile because sin is not only an act of rebellion against the law of God; it is also an act of hatred against the love of God.

This is precisely why King David, reflecting on his adultery, murder, and abuse of power, wrote about how his sins brought him no joy but instead caused his bones to feel crushed and his spirit sapped of joy (Ps. 51:8, 12). Going against the law and love of God tormented his soul, blocked his vision, sapped him with grief, and wasted him physically (Ps. 31:6–10).

To sin against the law of God is to sin against the love of God. Therefore, every time we sin against God, we also sin against ourselves. We cannot be happy and healthy and whole outside the blessed boundaries of God's law any more than a fish can be happy and healthy and whole outside of water. As those created in God's image, his law is our roadmap for how to "image" him. His law is our design and our most natural habitat. Eugene Peterson captures this truth well in his translation of Matthew 5:19: "Trivialize even the smallest item in God's Law and you will only have trivialized yourself" (MSG).

We Need Help Outside of Ourselves

Although the wisdom of adhering to our design may seem obvious, we desperately need help. Our hearts are deceptive, frail, and capable of justifying even our worst thoughts and words and actions. Our hearts are, like David's and Paul's, "prone to wander . . . prone to leave the God [we] love," to paraphrase the old hymn. We need the wisdom of Scripture daily to anchor us in things that are right, good, and true. Because we are not yet what we are meant to be, we need people in our lives to remind us that we have not arrived. We need honest voices helping us see the sin in ourselves that we cannot see and to confront us when we need confronting. Indeed, one of the most effective ways to discover our shortcomings is through the perspective and honest sharing—and especially the honest and forthright critique—of others. As Dietrich Bonhoeffer said, "Nothing can be more compassionate than the severe reprimand which calls another Christian in one's community back from the path of sin."[2]

It is difficult enough to accept correction from those *over* us in authority—our employers, teachers, parents, and elders. However, it can be especially tempting to shield ourselves from correction from those *under* our authority—our children, students, and employees. Our pride and self-sufficiency can fool us into believing that those under our authority have little to offer and no right to challenge. Yet, as people who wish to grow in grace and become more like Jesus Christ, it is vital that we listen and appropriately receive correction from those speaking truth to us. Those in authority will receive correction to the extent that they believe that they, too, are ultimately *under* authority—namely, the authority of Christ.

ALWAYS POISED AND READY TO REPENT

King David did not shield himself from hard truths. When Nathan the prophet confronted him for abusing his power through sexual exploitation and murder, David did not respond by saying, "Who do you think you are, Nathan? Do you have any idea who it is that you are talking to?"

Instead, David humbly received Nathan's rebuke, repented of his sin, and made restitution as he was able. And then he made one of the most comprehensive confessions of sin ever offered:

> Have mercy on me, O God, according to your steadfast love; according to your abundant mercy blot out my transgressions. Wash me thoroughly from my iniquity, and cleanse me from my sin! For I know my transgressions, and my sin is ever before me. Against you, you only, have I sinned and done what is evil

> in your sight . . . Behold, you delight in truth in the inward being, and you teach me wisdom in the secret heart . . . wash me, and I shall be whiter than snow . . . Hide your face from my sins . . . Create in me a clean heart, O God, and renew a right spirit within me. Cast me not away from your presence, and take not your Holy Spirit from me. Restore to me the joy of your salvation, and uphold me with a willing spirit. (Ps. 51:1–12)

First, David confessed his sin to God. He also confessed his sin to Nathan, saying, "I have sinned against the Lord." Then he turned to Bathsheba, the widowed wife of the soldier that he murdered, and became her husband.

In great mercy and kindness, God gave David and Bathsheba a son whose name, Jedediah, means *beloved of God*. This son was also given a second name, Solomon, which means *peace*. This gift of a son, born from circumstances involving horrific sin and abuse, would later be included in the ancestry of Jesus as a magnificent display of how long, wide, high, and deep the love of God travels: David was the father of Solomon by the wife of Uriah (Matt. 1:6).

Matthew goes out of his way to allude to the unsavory circumstances surrounding Solomon's birth. He could have easily said, "by Bathsheba" instead of "by the wife of Uriah." Instead, he uses an example from history to help us see how God worked to redeem the sin that David committed and from which he later repented.

And there was even more grace poured out on David. Jesus—the King of all kings and true Prince of Peace—would later identify himself as "the Son of David" and would call David "a man after [God's] own heart" (Acts 13:22 NIV).

There are many things we can learn from the life of David. One of the most important things is how essential it is to position ourselves to regularly receive critique from those around us—especially those who know us best, such as colleagues, friends, and family members—and also to receive it humbly, with gratitude, and with resoluteness to change. Our character must matter more to us than our reputations. We must learn to love the light, even when it exposes the darkness in us, as opposed to hiding from the light and shielding ourselves from exposure. We must pay careful attention to those parts of the Bible that we underline, but also and especially to those parts that we *don't* underline. We need a gentled posture before the Lord, his Word, and his truth-telling messengers, to become the people he desires for us to be.

And this, in spite of his many faults, was where David shined. The aftermath of the Bathsheba scandal presents a portrait of greatness—not because David was perfect, but because he was ready and willing to own his imperfection and to do so publicly. His greatness was found in his readiness to humble himself. In this, he shows us one of the key evidences that the Holy Spirit dwells within us: a willingness to lose face when one could easily save face. David was the one holding all the power, yet he expressed a readiness to repent even though he wasn't required to submit to anyone in his social and political ecosystem. David could have done the same thing to Nathan that he had done to Uriah—finish the man off, or at the very least keep him quiet and put him in his place, in order to save his own hide and reputation. But he did not. Instead, David chose to listen, humble himself, repent, and seek restoration.

The Final Proof of Greatness

Writer and philosopher Elbert Hubbard, a contemporary of Ralph Waldo Emerson, is believed to have said that the final proof of greatness lies in being able to endure criticism without resentment.[3] By this standard, David was a great man.

In the face of being confronted, why would David choose repentance rather than defensiveness and saving face? And why would we? For nothing less than the flourishing and health of our souls.

Think about it. We welcome the probing and scrutiny of our bodies by doctors. We give them access to our private parts. We say, "Yes, of course" when they ask to do an X-ray to evaluate our physical health. We let them examine, prick, and cut to prevent other greater wounds from destroying us. Why would we be any less receptive when it comes to allowing those closest to us the most intimate access to our conduct and character? Shouldn't we allow them—even invite them—to probe, prick, and wound us in order that our souls might be healed?

> Let a righteous man strike me—that is a kindness.
> (Ps. 141:5)
> Faithful are the wounds of a friend. (Prov. 27:6)
> Whoever brings back a sinner from his wandering will
> save his soul from death. (James 5:20)

Indeed, sometimes bringing out the best in someone includes lovingly exposing the worst in them. Sometimes adding to someone else's discomfort, as opposed to doing everything we can to keep everyone comfortable, can have the effect of helping their soul become stronger. *But do we believe this?*

As the following story illustrates, the same can apply to the times when we are confronted with ideas that cause us to feel threatened, provoked, offended, or unsafe. Depending on how we choose to respond to such ideas, we will contribute to making things better or worse in today's outrage culture.

In February 2017, political activist and former presidential adviser Van Jones gave an interview at the University of Chicago. The interviewer asked Jones about the escalating demand on college campuses that students be protected from ideas, perspectives, and speakers that make them feel uncomfortable. Rather than defend the idea of so-called safe spaces that allow students to escape ideas and speech that hurt their feelings, Jones decried the idea as damaging. In his view, today's students need to be challenged instead of coddled. Otherwise, they will be woefully unprepared for the world that they will soon enter as young adults, professionals, spouses, parents, and neighbors.

"There are two ideas about safe spaces," Jones said. "One is a very good idea, and one is a terrible idea." The good idea is "being physically safe on campus, not being subjected to sexual harassment and physical abuse. But there is another view that is now ascendant," Jones continued. "It's a horrible view, which is that 'I need to be safe ideologically, I need to be safe emotionally, I just need to feel good all the time. And if someone else says something that I don't like, that is a problem for everyone else, including the administration.'" He then declared, quite boldly, that safe spaces undermine the entire purpose of education, which is to teach students to think for themselves:

> I don't want you to be safe ideologically. I don't want you to be safe emotionally. I want you to be strong . . . I'm not going to pave the jungle for you. Put on some boots, and learn to deal with adversity. I'm not going to take all the weights out of the gym; that's the whole point of the gym . . . You can't live on a

> campus where people say stuff that you don't like? . . . [In] the real world [this] is not just useless but obnoxious and dangerous. I want you to be offended every single day on this campus. I want you to be deeply aggrieved and offended and upset and then learn how to speak back.[4]

As the great British statesman Winston Churchill said, social tension resulting from things like disagreement, ideas that offend us, and criticism is unpleasant; it is necessary for all of us. Why? "It fulfills the same function as pain in the human body; it calls attention to the development of an unhealthy state of things."[5]

When we resist uncomfortable ideas and criticism, especially fair criticism, we show ourselves to be unhealthy people. Unhealthy people, when criticized, tend to retreat, manipulate, or retaliate. People seeking health will tend to confess and repent.

WHEN THE CRITICISM IS UNFAIR

This raises some important questions. What if the criticism is unfair? What if the critic is someone who doesn't have our best interest in mind, but instead seems to have it out for us or is saying things about us that are not true? What if the critic, rather than aiming for our health and flourishing, is acting like a pig?

As King David illuminated how to respond to righteous correction from Nathan the prophet, he can also instruct us in how to respond in this story of an irritating man named Shimei. Shimei disliked how David was leading the people of Israel. He threw rocks at David and hurled insults at him, cursing him continually. David, once again having all the power, could have simply killed Shimei on the spot, and one of David's men longed to do precisely that:

> Abishai the son of Zeruiah said to the king, "Why should this dead dog curse my lord the king? Let me go over and take off his head." But the king said, ". . . If he is cursing because the LORD has said to him, 'Curse David,' who then shall say, 'Why have you done so?'" (2 Sam. 16:9–10)

According to my friend Scotty Smith who knew pastor and seminary professor Jack Miller in a close, personal way, Jack had a unique way of responding to critiques that were, in his opinion, unfair or even untrue. Miller said that whenever somebody criticized him unfairly or painted a negative caricature of him, he would turn to the person and say, "You don't know the half of it." Being aware of the darkness of his own heart enabled him to regard an unfair criticism as charitable compared to the true things about him, of which his critics were unaware. Miller became known for saying, "I am much worse than I think I am, and so are you."

I once heard a pastor tell a moving story about the evangelist Dwight L. Moody, who, while preaching the gospel to a large crowd, had his own "Shimei experience." A young, self-assured, know-it-all theological student in the crowd began to publicly challenge the things that Moody, the veteran evangelist, preached. The student rudely interrupted him several times and tried to trip him up. Eventually, Moody got fed up with the young man's rude behavior and snapped at him. The evangelist, widely known as one of the world's most eloquent communicators, used his gift with words to punish the young man, sharply putting him in his place in front of everyone. Thinking that the young man got what he deserved, the crowd showed their hearty approval of Moody's response. Then, later in his talk, Moody stopped himself and said in front of them all, "Friends, I have to confess before all of you that at the beginning of my meeting I gave a very foolish answer to my brother down here. I ask God to forgive me, and I ask him to forgive me."

Moody demonstrated true leadership and greatness in that moment. Though he could have said nothing and gone home satisfied that he had soundly defeated the young antagonist in their public standoff, he instead humbled himself and publicly apologized. He, the one "in power," valued his character and the young man in front of him more than he valued saving face. Though guilty of the seemingly *lesser* sin, he became the *first* to repent and apologize.

Pastor Tim Keller once posted a tweet that said, "Even if only 20% is true, we can profit from criticism given by people who are badly motivated or whom we don't respect."[6] I served alongside Tim for several years in New York City and can personally attest that Tim is much more than talk on these matters.

Over the course of his life and large ministry, Tim has received plenty of public criticism. Instead of bringing out the worst in him, receiving criticism seems to have brought out the best in him. His usual response is not the typical retaliatory or defensive response we've come to expect in our current climate. Instead, he responds with self-reflective, humble, and gentle answers. Tim's words and example have been helpful to me in times that I've also been criticized for things I've said or done in service to the cause of Christ. He has become a picture for me of how even the worst criticisms can provide fresh opportunities to draw near to Christ, and as we do, to imitate Christ's own gentle response. Tim wrote:

> If the criticism comes from someone who doesn't know you at all [and often this is the case on the internet] it is possible that the criticism is completely unwarranted and profoundly mistaken. I am often pilloried not only for views I do have, but also even more often for views [and motives] that I do not hold at all. When that happens, it is even easier to fall into a smugness and perhaps be tempted to laugh at how mistaken your critics are. "Pathetic . . ." you may be tempted to say. Don't do it. Even if there is not the slightest kernel of truth in what the critic says, you should not mock them in your thoughts. First, remind yourself of examples of your own mistakes, foolishness, and cluelessness in the past, times in which you really got something wrong. Second, pray for the critic, that he or she grows in grace.[7]

In 2017, Keller was awarded the esteemed Kuyper Prize at the Abraham Kuyper Center for Public Theology at Princeton Theological Seminary—until he was not. The prize, given to a single recipient annually since 1998, was designated to Keller for the excellence with which he has consistently modeled application of Kuyper's theology that declares God's ownership of "every square inch" (as Kuyper himself put it) of the created universe. Whether in business, the arts, politics, journalism, or other areas of influence, Keller has encouraged and empowered men and women to integrate their faith and their work, such that the lordship of Christ is brought to bear not only in private religious spaces, but also in public spheres of influence and the marketplace of ideas. Keller's application of Kuyper in his teaching and ministry has been so pervasive over the years that he was named in *Fortune* magazine's 2018 "World's 50 Greatest Leaders" list.[8]

Although Keller was more than qualified for the Kuyper Prize, a backlash arose from several students and faculty in the Princeton community after the announcement occurred that he would be the esteemed recipient. The backlash was related to Keller's views on sex, marriage, and women's ordination, which sit on the historic-traditional side of the theological continuum. As a result of the complaints the seminary received, the award was rescinded and instead given to a recipient who represented Princeton's majority views on these matters.

Nevertheless, the Kuyper Center asked Keller, who was no longer to be the recipient of the award based on criteria that would have also eliminated Abraham Kuyper himself from consideration, to lecture at the conference where the award was given to someone else. Keller, harboring zero resentment or hard feelings, graciously agreed.[9]

In an op-ed following Princeton's announcement to retract the award given to Keller, Katherine Alsdorf, cofounder of New York City's Center for Faith and Work, reflected on the announcement:

> [Tim and I] partnered in the establishment of the Center for Faith and Work, which may have done as much as any church in decades to honor Abraham Kuyper's vision of humble, respectful engagement in a world of many faith perspectives. His teaching combines a deep confidence that the gospel can change everything from our hearts, making us more humble and generous, to the institutions and society around us. While he would never have sought a "Kuyper award," I can't imagine anyone more worthy of it.
>
> Like some of the women who have objected and instigated the withdrawal of this award by Princeton Theological

> Seminary, I do not share Tim's complementarian views. However, I am deeply saddened by the tone of these objections, more so by the final effect.[10]

Depending on our particular perspective, we will all be moved in different ways by stories like this one. As for me, I am both touched and inspired by Keller's remarkable graciousness, as well as Alsdorf's humble, mature willingness to accept leadership from Keller for a higher good, even though they are not in full agreement even on things that are deeply important to them both. Each of them, in his or her own way, demonstrates for us what a gentle answer that comes from Christ can look like.

TRUTH-TELLING, OLIVE BRANCHES, AND OUR CRITICS

As we consider our call from Jesus to offer a gentle answer in the face of criticism and discord, it may be helpful to pause and paint one final picture of what such a response could look like. What follows is a fictitious letter, written by a hypothetical man named "David" to a hypothetical critic whom we will call "Shim-Than." This name, Shim-Than, combines the name of King David's unfair critic, Shimei, with the name of his fair critic, Nathan. I'm combining the two because, as in the case of David, even unfair criticism calls for careful consideration and a gracious response. Even unfair criticism should be examined for kernels of truth that present new opportunities for repenting and drawing near to Jesus. And often both unfair and fair critiques can come together, bound up into one.

Although the following letter is hypothetical, I imagine that many readers will be able to see themes that intersect with their own lives, experiences, and fractured relationships. Hopefully the letter will provide a helpful picture of what it can look like to respond to criticism with gentleness, truth, and grace.

Dear Shim-Than,

I write for a reason that may surprise you—chiefly to say thanks.

First, I want to thank you for our many years of friendship before the recent breakdown occurred. Whether it be our shared love for Scripture and books, the local church, delicious BBQ, a good movie, the St. Louis Cardinals, or the company where we've both worked for years, you have been a kindred spirit to me. Thank you also for the times you have supported me as leader of our team at work, as well as in my marriage and parenting and in my growth as a Christian. Though I have been your boss, for many years I have looked up to you as an example in the areas of family and faith.

Thank you for how you've sometimes extended kindness to me personally. When our whole family had the flu, you surprised us with meals—what employee does that for his boss's family? Sometimes when I felt discouraged and under pressure at work, you encouraged me to hang in there and affirmed my leadership. Even when things started to become tense between us, you remained honoring, deferential, and kind. Thank you for your many thoughtful notes and generous words over the years that came at just the right time, especially after my mother died.

Although you are younger than I am, I have always

appreciated and learned from the way that you honor your wife. You speak of her with such esteem, and it's obvious how much you love and respect her. Your example in this makes me want to love and respect my wife, Bathsheba, even more than I already do. Marriage is a powerful conduit of grace, especially when the Lord and his gospel are its foundation. Of this, you and your wife have been among our foremost teachers—and given our past and sometimes current struggles, we have surely needed it.

Shim-Than, I am also deeply saddened that our friendship has faded. I am hurt by your recent and uncharacteristic criticisms of my leadership to our colleagues, as well as the related things you've insinuated about my character and integrity. I am hurt that you have taken your grievances public, even airing them to my boss, to some of our mutual friends at church, and once or twice on social media. And you did this, Shim-Than, without ever approaching me personally. The closest you ever came to doing so was through a long e-mail after the damage had already been done through your gossip. I can't help but wonder if, had you approached me personally, our apparent differences would have never escalated to the level of tension that they have.

Even though I believe you have mischaracterized my leadership and character in the things you have said about me, in e-mails you have written, and now on social media, I am nevertheless thankful for some of the outcomes the Lord has brought about through your critiques.

As I've processed your criticisms, I want to also acknowledge that each of us, myself included, can benefit from an opposing voice every now and then. As you and I have discussed many times over a beer or breakfast or coffee, it is sometimes the contrarians who make things better instead of worse. Dietrich Bonhoeffer was a contrarian in his opposition to Hitler, Martin Luther in his opposition to the sins and abuses of the church, Mother Teresa in her opposition to the conditions of poverty and starvation, Newton and Wilberforce in their opposition to the slave trade, Martin Luther King Jr. in his opposition to racism and inequality, Sojourner Truth in her opposition to slavery, and the many church councils in their opposition to heretical teachings and ideas.

Sometimes it takes opposition to stir the pot, to challenge a broken status quo, and to fight for needed change—this includes everything from political systems to office cultures to church communities to family systems to individual human hearts. Even though others at work have never criticized me in the ways or level of intensity that you have, that does not necessarily mean that everything you've said is wrong. The minority voice sometimes has the most helpful and most important things to say. So even though I feel you have injured me, I am seeking to learn from this whole sad and hurtful experience.

Shim-Than, I don't fault you for following your convictions or telling it like you see it. I am reminded through scripture, prayer, and life experience that I am in reality much worse than anything you or anybody else could say about me. As Jack Miller used to say to his fair and unfair critics, "You don't know the half of it." I am quite aware that left to myself and apart from grace, I deserve nothing besides the judgment and disfavor of God. My sins are too many to count; God's mercies are more still. I am a great sinner, but Christ is an even greater Savior. I rejoice in his kindness and patience toward me—as well as his delight to use me in his service through whatever means he chooses—the awareness of which your critiques have brought to the forefront of my mind and heart.

One of my older mentor-bosses, also a believer like us, taught me to repent and make amends quickly when criticized fairly, and, when criticized unfairly, to look for a kernel of truth in hopes of finding something to repent of. This draws us closer to Christ and enables us to remove a speck from our critic's eye. However, even then, one should consider showing restraint, for it is often best to leave the "ministry of speck removal" to the Holy Spirit.

Your critiques—whether fair or unfair is for the Lord to decide—have led me toward introspection and intentionality about growing in the Spirit's fruit of both faithfulness and gentleness. In all my work, I want to be found faithful. In all my responses to criticism such as yours—whether fair or unfair—I want to respond in a spirit of humility and meekness. Your critiques have sparked my desire to pursue peace with others, to humble myself in the sight of the Lord, to get and stay low, to seek God in prayer, and to be a servant. For this, I thank you.

My practice for many years has been to ask God to give me character that is greater than my gifts, and humility that is greater than my influence. I ask God daily to search my heart, to test me, to correct any and every offensive way in me, and to lead me in the way everlasting. Even though you have distanced yourself from me personally, and even though I do not recognize my own behaviors, motivations, and work ethic in most of the ways that you have characterized them, I would ask you to pray for me that I would grow in my ability to live and lead in a humble and faithful manner, even as one who is still in process.

And I will continue to pray for you.

Shim-Than, I have no idea how you will receive this letter. I do hope that in some way it will be a source of encouragement for you, as well as a gesture toward reconciliation and peace. This is my prayer, and it is the reason why I believe the Lord put it on my heart to write to you.

I wish the very best for you and those that you love.

Your brother in Christ,
David

QUESTIONS FOR REFLECTION AND DISCUSSION

1. Name one thing from this chapter that troubled you, inspired you, or both. Why were you impacted in this way?
2. When you are criticized, what is your typical response? In what ways has the experience of being criticized revealed in you a need for growth? In what ways has the experience shown that the Lord is actively at work in you? How is your usual response to criticism similar to David's response to Shim-Than? How is it different?
3. What are your thoughts regarding Tim Keller's perspective on receiving criticism? What, if anything, makes his response difficult for you?
4. Based on this chapter, identify one way that the Lord might be nudging you toward growth or change. What steps should you take to pursue the change?

SEVEN

We Forgive All the Way

This week, a disturbing article landed in my in-box. According to the article, a well-known pastor allegedly sought the services of a hitman on two separate occasions in order to kill two people. The first alleged target was a critic of his ministry. The second was his former son-in-law.

As I read the article, I felt emotions ranging from bewilderment to confusion to judgment to anger. How on earth could a man called to ministry—whose job it is to mirror the kindness and love of God—develop a grudge so deep that he would take measures not only to injure someone, but to murder? How far gone in his soul does someone have to be to get to this point? And how will this sort of story, when added to the many other stories of abuse, adultery, deceit, and financial indiscretion among church leaders, reflect Jesus and the gospel to a watching world? How will it reflect on the already tarnished reputation of ministers, once regarded as the most trustworthy profession in our society, but whose trustworthiness is now at an all-time low?[1]

Then I began to reflect on Jesus' words from the Sermon on the Mount: "You have heard that it was said to those of old, 'You shall not murder; and whoever murders will be liable to judgment,'" he said. "But I say to you that everyone who is angry with his brother will be liable to judgment . . . and whoever says, 'You fool!' will be liable to the hell of fire" (Matt. 5:21–22).

For obvious reasons, it is easy for us to be appalled when we hear that a pastor would seek out the services of a hitman. But are we also appalled when *character* assassination through gossip and slander occurs in churches, restaurants, living rooms, and on the Internet? In God's eyes, while one certainly has more far-reaching consequences than the other, both seeking out a partner in gossip and seeking out a hitman come from similar roots. I say this not to diminish the seriousness of hiring a hitman, but rather to draw attention to the fact that resentful seeds reside in every human heart. These seeds can grow and become evil desires to hurt or take down another.

In chapter 5, we looked at two different forms of anger: righteous and unrighteous. But that raises a question: What keeps our anger righteous? There is a practice, cultivated in cooperation with the Holy Spirit, that can help us do so, while also embodying and advancing the gentleness of Jesus Christ in our dealings with others who have injured us. This specific form of heart work is an essential prerequisite to all forms of healthy, righteous anger. Without it, the kind of gentleness that turns away wrath simply cannot exist. Christian discipleship gets derailed without it, because its absence negates what scripture calls the "ministry of reconciliation" (see 2 Cor. 5:11–21), a ministry God does through us for the purpose of demolishing dividing walls of enmity and strife.

What is this specific practice that is such an essential component of healthy conflict and reconciliation? It's the virtue and practice of maintaining a forgiving posture, enabling us to forgive others as God in Christ has forgiven us (Eph. 4:32).

THE GRACE TO FORGIVE IS A COSTLY, GUTSY GRACE

In his famous Sermon on the Mount, Jesus taught his disciples and us to pray, "Forgive us our debts, as we also have forgiven our debtors." Then he continued, "For if you forgive others their trespasses, your heavenly Father will also forgive you, but if you do not forgive others their trespasses, neither will your Father forgive your trespasses" (Matt. 6:12, 14–15). Clearly, forgiveness is a foundational, significant part of our relationship with God and others.

When separated from broader context, it sounds like Jesus is saying that there is a cause-effect relationship between our forgiveness of others and God's willingness to forgive us. What a disorienting thought, that God's acceptance of me is based on my ability to forgive others. However, within the broader context of Jesus' words and the New Testament's teaching, it's clear that such a conclusion is unwarranted. Salvation, which includes receiving and experiencing God's forgiveness, is by grace through faith in Christ alone. It is not based upon works of any kind, including the work of forgiving others (Eph. 2:8–9). Only the work of Jesus is able to save us.

Jesus is not saying that the Father's saving grace is given as a result of one's works of forgiveness. However, Jesus *is* saying that if we prefer our grudges over pursuing reconciliation, either we are stunted in our Christian growth or we might not be Christian at all. Do we prefer to remain at odds with an enemy versus doing the work of making peace with them? Do we prefer to resent and retaliate, instead of forgiving those who have injured us? Is being vindictive more appealing to us than being merciful and kind? Have we become *the kinds of people* for whom resentment feels justified and a gentle answer feels insufficient?

Counselor Dan Allender wrote, "We have to ponder, to search our hearts [about why we cannot forgive]. The labor of such a search means we may be in for the wild ride of facing our hidden demands, concealed wounds, and camouflaged pettiness. The discovery of our self-righteousness may be a nightmare. It might expose a cruel, miserly, Scrooge-like heart."[2]

Self-examination, however, is not enough, according to Allender. He explains that forgiveness involves wanting the best for the offender, observing that "forgiving love is the inconceivable, unexplainable pursuit of the offender by the offended for the sake of restored relationship with God, self, and others . . . I will not be able to love unless I forgive; and I will not forgive unless my hatred is continually melted by the searing truth and grace of the gospel. True biblical forgiveness is a glorious gift for both the offender and the offended."[3]

Not for the Faint of Heart

After hearing Jesus teach about pursuing reconciliation and forgiveness, Peter asks him a clarifying question. "Lord, how often will my brother sin against me, and I forgive him? As many as seven times?" (Matt. 18:21).

Before we condemn Peter for being stingy in the application

of grace toward others, and before we conclude that he lacks gentleness and mercy, we should first consider the limits of our own patience toward repeat offenses and offenders. How often have *we* been unwilling to forgive others, even for small offenses? And if that consideration isn't enough to have some sympathy for Peter's response, we should better understand the Jewish teaching and expectations of Peter's day.

Peter was familiar with the teaching that if a person sinned against you once or twice, you must forgive them. After the third time, forgiveness was no longer required. In comparison to this norm, Peter was saying that he would be all-in, even if the Lord wanted him to more than double the rabbis' forgiveness standards. Peter was willing to go far above and beyond what even the rabbis commanded concerning forgiveness because of his love and loyalty to Jesus.

Jesus' answer to Peter was surprising, because he took forgiveness to an even higher level. "I do not say to you seven times," Jesus said, "but seventy-seven times" (Matt. 18:22). This phrase, seventy-seven times, was an idiom that implied an infinite number. The rabbis' requirement to forgive three times was not enough. Peter's willingness to forgive more than twice this number also fell short. According to Jesus, if we want to be his disciples, then we must not place any limits on the number of times we are willing to forgive those who offend, insult, injure, persecute, and betray us. This includes smaller, innocuous offenses such as a driver cutting us off in traffic, a restaurant server getting our food order wrong, or a person criticizing our political views. It also includes greater offenses, the ones that feel like the ripping of our flesh and the crushing of our spirits.

Forgiving others as God in Christ has forgiven us is gutsy and gut-wrenching, courageous and terrifying, redemptive and messy, breathtaking and exhausting, and heavenly and hellish in what it is going to require of us.

This practice of forgiveness is no easy endeavor.

The Forgiving Saints of Old

The Bible offers several examples of what forgiving seventy-seven times can look like. We are told of Joseph, who was betrayed and sold into slavery by his older brothers. Years later when they were finally called upon to face him, Joseph comforted them and said, "As for you, you meant evil against me, but God meant it for good, to bring it about that many people should be kept alive, as they are today" (Gen. 50:20).

We are told of Hosea, the prophet of Israel who was called upon by God to marry Gomer, who would betray him over and over again through adultery. Instead of divorcing her, which would be entirely justified due to her serial infidelity, Hosea forgave and pursued her repeatedly. Hosea's gentleness and faithful forgiveness gave God's people a visible picture of what it looks like for God to repeatedly forgive their many infidelities, to pursue and promise to betroth himself to them forever, and to never leave or forsake them (Hos. 2:19; Heb. 13:5).

We are told of the prophet Isaiah, whose preaching was denounced and scorned by every person in Israel, including those who would execute him by sawing him in two. Instead of resenting and retaliating against those who rejected him, Isaiah offered assurances such as, "Come now, let us reason together, says the Lord: though your sins are like scarlet, they shall be as white as snow; though they are red like crimson, they shall become like wool" (Isa. 1:18) and "As a young man marries a young woman . . .

and as the bridegroom rejoices over the bride, so shall your God rejoice over you" (Isa. 62:5).

We are told of the martyr Stephen, who prayed for his killers as they hurled flesh-piercing, skull-crushing rocks at his head. As they rushed toward him and sneered at him through gritted teeth, Stephen looked toward heaven and said, "Lord Jesus, receive my spirit . . . do not hold this sin against them" (Acts 7:54–60).

We are told of the apostle Paul, who presided over this same Stephen's death prior to his own conversion to Christianity. Having been forgiven for the great evil he had done, he would later say that if it were possible, he would be willing to even give up his own salvation if that's what it took for God to save those who were wishing *him* dead. "I have great sorrow and unceasing anguish in my heart," Paul wrote. "For I could wish that I myself were accursed and cut off from Christ for the sake of my brothers, my kinsmen according to the flesh" (Rom. 9:2–3).

There is something remarkable about the extent to which people were willing to forgive after they themselves had tasted God's forgiveness toward them.

Jonah, the Resentful Saint

Scripture also gives us a look at what *not* forgiving looks like in the four chapters of Jonah. God gave Jonah a challenging, significant task: to preach God's love to the people of Nineveh in hopes that the whole city, including their tyrannical king, would listen, be humbled, repent, and be saved. For years, Assyria's capital city, Nineveh, had only been known by Jonah and his fellow Jews as oppressive, abusive, and violent. Assyria's scorched-earth expansion through military force, torture, rape, and enslavement had brutally and systematically wrecked many lives and communities.

The prophet had zero interest in being part of God's rescue mission to this evil, undeserving city. His only interest toward Nineveh was resentment, hatred, scorn, and, if the opportunity ever presented itself, retaliation and revenge toward a violent and inhumane people.

Forgive and preach grace to them? You've got to be kidding me!

As C. S. Lewis said, "Everyone says forgiveness is a lovely idea until they have something to forgive."[4]

Jonah had no desire to forgive Nineveh or to see them forgiven. Instead, he wanted to see them utterly and mercilessly destroyed. But Jonah's resentful grudge toward Nineveh ended up injuring him much more than it injured them. It caused him to become fixated on his own resentment and victimhood, proving that the true prisoner of a grudge is not the one against whom it is held, but the one who does the holding. In Jonah's case and in ours, "contemptuous actions and attitudes are a knife in the heart that permanently harms and mutilates people's souls."[5]

Like a poisonous berry, vindictiveness tastes sweet and swallows smoothly at first. But once it gets into you, it starts working less like fruit and more like cyanide. To survive it, we must expunge it from our system.

It costs us dearly to forgive somebody.

It costs us even more *not* to forgive.

ANCIENT PATHS FOR MODERN INJURIES

On June 17, 2015, the members of a small black church in Charleston, South Carolina, were faced with Jesus difficult and costly teaching on forgiveness. During a midweek Bible study and prayer meeting, a young Caucasian man named Dylann Roof walked in to the meeting, introduced himself, and then took out an automatic weapon and opened fire on the congregants. In total, nine of the victims died from Roof's violent, senseless, and racially motivated rampage.

Less than two years after the incident, several of Roof's victims, as well as friends and families of those who had been killed, were given an opportunity to address him in court. Felicia Sanders, whose son was one of the murder victims, said to the killer, "You took my love away from me . . . I know you because you are in my head all day . . . I forgive you. May God have mercy on your soul." Tyrone Sanders, the deceased boy's father, likewise said, "Why you want to single out black people in church, I don't know. But whoever your creator is needs to come be with you." Bethany Middleton Brown, whose sister was a murder victim, said, "I wanted to hate you, but my faith tells me no. I wanted to remain angry and bitter, but my view of life won't let me."

After the last statement was made by the victims' friends and loved ones, Roof, who never made eye contact with those who addressed him, offered a short and chilling closing statement in response. "I still feel like I had to do it," the unremorseful killer said.[6]

As this horrific and maddening account reveals, forgiving from the heart often does not provide emotional closure to the forgiver. In cases where the perpetrator shows no remorse, those injured by his actions are placed in the agonizing position of having to absorb the emotional impact of the injury until the day when Jesus returns to right every wrong, to heal every hurt, and to call to account every injury that has been inflicted by humans on other humans. As the Apostles' Creed reminds us, Jesus Christ "will come to judge the living and the dead." While attorneys and courtrooms and criminal justice systems mete out appropriate consequences for injurious criminal behavior, nothing in this world can pay down the emotional toll of malice and betrayal.

Miroslav Volf is a professor of theology and founder of the Yale Center for Faith and Culture. He also understands the gut-wrenching nature of what is required of Christians as they forgive in the way that they have been forgiven. Having grown up in war-torn Croatia, Volf is uncomfortably familiar with the soul-crushing violence in the Balkan region. As such, he is painfully aware of the physical and emotional toll of vengeance and retaliation cycles.

In his masterful book, *Exclusion and Embrace,* Volf suggested that people enact vengeance on other people not because they believe in God's judgment, but because they don't. Atheism and agnosticism, Volf said, are far more potent contributors to the cycle of vengeance than belief in God and his judgment. According to his logic, if there is no God and therefore no judgment, then human beings have nowhere to go with pain that has been inflicted upon them by others. If there is no God and no judgment, our only options are to suffer the injury of injustice on our own or to fight back in retaliation. Whichever route we choose, the results are tragic and ultimately devastating. Only belief in a God who will come to judge the living and the dead, Volf contended, will enable believers to stop the cycle of violence, and to entrust themselves to the One who judges justly, as Jesus did (see 1 Peter 2:23). Volf wrote:

> The only means of prohibiting all recourse to violence by ourselves is to insist that violence is legitimate only when it

> comes from God . . . My thesis that the practice of nonviolence requires a belief in divine vengeance will be unpopular with many Christians . . . Soon you would discover that it takes the quiet of a suburban home for the birth of the thesis that human nonviolence corresponds to God's refusal to judge. In a scorched land, soaked in the blood of the innocent, it will invariably die. And as one who watches it die, one will do well to reflect about many other pleasant captivities of the liberal mind.[7]

As one who had experienced and witnessed horrific injustices, Volf believed that perspective and experience change everything. When enemies have destroyed your home, murdered, and in some cases raped your family members, there is no way to handle the pain unless you kill yourself to end the anguish, kill your heart to numb the emotional vandalism, or entrust yourself to the God who will come to judge the living and the dead.

A recent and courageous example of what it looks like for a victim to entrust herself to the God who judges justly is Rachael Denhollander. A former Michigan State University gymnast, Denhollander spoke in court in January 2018 at the sentencing of Larry Nassar, an athletic trainer and therapist who had systematically sexually abused woman athletes for years. Denhollander, one of his many victims and also a Christian, said the following to the defendant:

> If you have read the Bible . . . you know that the definition of sacrificial love portrayed is of God himself loving so sacrificially that he gave up everything to pay a penalty for the sin that he did not commit. By his grace, I, too, choose to love this

> way . . . you have damaged hundreds . . . The Bible . . . carries a final judgment where all of God's wrath and its eternal terror is poured out on men like you . . . And that is what makes the gospel of Christ so sweet because it extends grace and hope and mercy where none should be found. And it will be there for you.[8]

As she concluded her remarks, Denhollander told Nassar that she forgives him, but that more than anything else in the world he needs forgiveness from God. In making such prophetic and inspired remarks, the gymnast-victim-turned-hero reminds us that forgiveness in Christ is available for all who hear the voice of the Lord, even for the worst perpetrators.

To extend forgiving grace involves truth-telling and maintaining a non-retaliatory posture. "Beloved, never avenge yourselves, but leave it to the wrath of God, for it is written, 'Vengeance is mine, I will repay, says the Lord'" (Rom. 12:19). As we extend the forgiveness that Christ has secured for us, we open our hearts to the possibility, even to the hope, that the offending party would someday soften and experience sorrow for the hurt he has caused. We also hold out hope that the perpetrator would confess his wrongdoing and seek forgiveness from God and from us. Our forgiveness includes the ongoing choice of exchanging our daydreams of our enemy's demise for new daydreams, ones in which he is humbled into repentance in such a way that even safe, appropriate, relational restoration and repair is made possible.

This is what happened to Saul of Tarsus when he was converted to faith in Christ. The one who once sought to capture and kill the followers of Christ would become, over time, a cherished friend and brother and father to all. The one who had once been "a blasphemer, persecutor, and insolent opponent" would later receive mercy and grace from God. And he would receive the same from those he had once sought out to harm (see Acts 9:1–19; 1 Tim. 1:12–16).

A VIRTUE NEEDING CLEAR DEFINITION

Reflecting on injuries inflicted upon him as a result of racism and injustice, black educator and reformer Booker T. Washington is quoted as saying, "I would permit no man, no matter what his colour might be, to narrow and degrade my soul by making me hate him."[9]

It is inspiring to read such words from an iconic hero. It is quite another thing when we personally experience deep hurt and injury to the degree that we are tempted to hate. Some offenses are especially cruel and painful. We need the grace of God undergirding us and a supportive community surrounding us. This context enables us to understand more clearly what forgiveness is and what it is not.

Forgiveness Is Not Acting Like a Doormat

Forgiving others for insult and injury does not require us to be doormats. It is not letting the offending party off the hook. It is not withholding accountability or the appropriate expressions of anger toward the offender. We are not called to be passive or to allow ourselves to be taken advantage of. In fact, scripture forbids that we be doormats as it instructs us, "Be angry and do not sin" (Eph. 4:26). When we are sinned against, certain forms of anger are actually signs of gospel virtue. We are called into a careful dance between righteous anger on the one hand and forgiving grace on the other.

While they may want to humbly extend grace, Christians might misunderstand and misapply Jesus' teaching on non-retaliation. "You have heard that it was said, 'An eye for an eye and a tooth for a tooth.' But I say to you, Do not resist the one who is evil. But if anyone slaps you on the right cheek, turn to him the other also. And if anyone would sue you and take your tunic, let him have your cloak as well" (Matt. 5:38–40).

A misreading of this text might lead an abused spouse to conclude that she should keep taking the abuse, or that a falsely accused inmate should not ask an attorney to plead his case, or that a bullied student should keep being bullied instead of standing up for herself. As humans and as Christians, the Lord did not intend for us to be passive in such situations. There is a righteous anger and a healthy response that goes along with forgiveness and a gentle answer. When we are targets and victims of someone else's sin, we must find the healthy ways to make it difficult for others to continue sinning against us, just as Rachael Denhollander did with her abuser. It is, in other words, a very *Christian* thing to say to an offender, "Enough is enough!"

Forgiveness Is Not Automatic Trust

Forgiving those who have injured is not easy work, and it is not for the faint of heart. Depending on the degree of injury, the process can be excruciating. Even when sorrow has been expressed by the offending party, it may take the person or persons injured a significant amount of time to regain trust.

If an unfaithful husband is repentant and remorseful of his adultery, his wife may seek to pursue reconciliation instead of suing for divorce. However, this does not mean that she immediately owes him her trust. Especially when such serious betrayal has occurred, the husband must not expect his wife to trust him until there has been enough time for him to develop restored patterns of being trustworthy. Even after the husband has apologized, personally owned what he has done, and renewed his vow to be faithful to his wife as long as they both shall live, he must allow her time to trust him fully again. While she must not begrudge him or use past behavior as leverage against him in future disagreements, she will also need the grace of time for her wounds to be healed and her trust to be restored.

Forgiveness Is Canceling the Offender's Debt

In the parable of the unmerciful servant, we see what it means to forgive as God in Christ has forgiven us—or rather what it looks like *not* to do so. As the parable tells us, a king, out of pity for a servant who owed him more than he could ever repay, released the servant and canceled his debt (Matt. 18:27). Yet this same man then refused to cancel a much lesser debt of a fellow servant, and instead threw him into prison. He had been forgiven much, yet he refused to extend mercy and forgiveness to another. We, too, are faced with the choice to exercise vengeance or extend mercy. Blind bitterness demands payment, while forgiveness beckons us to relinquish our assumed right to retaliate against our offender.

A beautiful example of this kind of forgiveness is pictured in Victor Hugo's masterpiece, *Les Miserables*. In the novel, Jean Valjean is a homeless ex-convict who takes shelter under the hospitable roof of Bishop Myriel. Any visitors to Myriel's home "found nothing remarkable except two candlesticks of an antiquated design on the mantelpiece, which were presumably silver."

Besides the two candlesticks, the bishop was a modest man not given to excess, who had poured his life out in service and generosity toward others.

Despite being given generous provision and care, Valjean ruthlessly steals the bishop's silverware and silver plates and runs from the bishop's home in the dark of night. The police soon find Valjean and demand that the silver be returned to its rightful owner before they haul him off to prison. The bishop's grace and generosity rise to new heights as Valjean is brought before him and expects accusation and arrest. Instead of identifying Valjean as the betrayer and thief, the bishop extends forgiveness. He calmly tells the police that there has been a mistake, and that the silver was actually given to Valjean as a gift. He goes on to explain that Valjean had been careless in forgetting to take the candlesticks as well. As Valjean stands in disbelief and confusion, the bishop hands him the precious candlesticks to prove to the officers that no crime has been committed. To seal the deal, the bishop instructs Valjean to use the money from the sale of the silver and candlesticks to start living a better and more virtuous life. The bishop's sacrificial actions go beyond justice to mercy.

The novel goes on to depict how Valjean, once a miserable and desperate thief, is redeemed and restored by the bishop's gracious extension of forgiveness. The broken man is radically transformed and becomes an honest businessman, benefactor, and friend. In the final scene of the book, Valjean passes away in a room illuminated by just two candles, each held by one of the candlesticks that had been graciously given to him by Bishop Myriel. As he breathed his last, he "lay back with his head turned to the sky, and the light from the two candlesticks fell upon his face."[10]

This relationship between priest and thief in *Les Miserables* provides a moving picture of the forgiveness we ourselves have received from Jesus Christ, who spared no expense to cancel our debt, release us from the chains we deserve, and let us go free. The forgiveness that we have received becomes the forgiveness that we must share. This is part of the vision that inspired the black church members in Charleston to forgive a racist shooter or Rachael Denhollander to forgive her abuser.

Forgiveness Is Compelled by Pity

When the servant begged the king for mercy, the king canceled his insurmountable debt and let him go. The reason he did this is the same reason God cancels our debt and lets us go. He did so "out of pity for him" (Matt. 18:27).

To pity an offender is to discern the truth that beneath every sin and offense, there is also a wound. It is a God-given *sorrow* on behalf of all parties involved, including the ones who have done most of the injuring, that compels us to forgive from the heart when we or somebody we love has been injured. In Scripture, God demonstrates immense love and patience and forgiveness to serious offenders including leaders with a temper like Moses, weak husbands like Abraham, unfair fathers like Isaac, liars like Jacob, resentful runaway prophets like Jonah, prostitutes like Gomer and Rahab, adulterers and murderers and abusers of power like David, womanizers like Solomon, big mouths like Peter, crooks like Zacchaeus, demoniacs like Mary Magdalene, and the list goes on.

It helps to be reminded that in this tired world filled with sin and all of sin's collateral pain, it is hurting people who tend to do most of the hurting of others. It is a vicious cycle that can be broken only through the grace of God and by the power of Jesus Christ. Many who are sexually immoral were once victims of sexual abuse, many abusive bosses and spouses and parents were abused themselves in childhood, many who have difficulty committing are also children of divorce, and many who tell lies have themselves been lied to.

While these factors do not excuse a person for causing pain to others, they are nonetheless a helpful reminder that beneath most distorted human behavior are wounds that influence it—wounds that can heal when met with a gentle answer from Christ and from his people, as opposed to bitter, retaliatory responses. Nowhere in scripture does it say that it is repentance that causes God to be kind. On the contrary, scripture insists that it is the kindness of God that leads us to repent (Rom. 2:4).

AN IMPOSSIBLE VIRTUE MADE POSSIBLE

We can look again to the parable of the unmerciful servant for the reasons and motives that make forgiveness possible. The king in the parable initially cracks down on his servant, a man who owes him ten thousand talents, which in today's currency is somewhere near six billion dollars. Even though the king knew that this servant would never be able to repay him, he was moved by compassion, canceled the debt, and let the man go free. After the king forgives the servant of this whopping amount, the redeemed servant turns around and tosses a fellow servant into prison for not being able to immediately pay to *him* a debt of one hundred denarii, our modern equivalent of about twelve thousand dollars.

Twelve thousand dollars is a significant amount of money,

but compared to six billion dollars, it's a mere drop in the bucket. Bishop N. T. Wright once said that God has forgiven each of us a bucket filled to the brim with water, and in turn requires that we forgive others a total amounting to a single drop from that same bucket. We have received immense and immeasurable kindness from the Lord. The fellowship of the Father, Son, and Holy Spirit was ruptured as Jesus Christ went to his death to pay the sin debt that we owed and could never repay. He was literally "liquidated" of his own lifeblood as an act of supreme pity through which he canceled our debt and let us go free. In light of such rich mercy, how could we not extend mercy to our fellow human beings?

Our problem, Wright suggests, is that we see ourselves as merely ordinary sinners, but we see others as extreme sinners. We are favorable to God extending lavish grace toward us, yet we are stingy when we discover that God wants us to extend *his* grace through us to someone else.[11] As Miroslav Volf wrote in reference to the soul-crushing cycle of violence in the Balkan region, "Forgiveness flounders because I exclude the enemy from the community of humans even as I exclude myself from the community of sinners."[12]

The Cross Reveals Both Our Debt and Our Value

No one deserves forgiveness. While we were *still* sinners is precisely when Christ died for us. Not when we were doing good, but when we were up to no good. Not when we had a lot to offer God, but when we had empty hands. Not when we pulled ourselves up by the moral bootstraps, but when we had no boots to put on our feet. Not when we acted as his friends, but when we acted as his enemies. That is why Jesus Christ bled out for us on the cross, crying out to a God who for the first time ever turned a deaf ear to him, "My God, my God, why have you forsaken me?" (Ps. 22:1; Matt. 27:46). There is relief and joy to have and to extend when we are able to recognize how supremely loved we are by Jesus Christ.

When someone injures us and we are tempted to injure in return, it is crucial that we remember the answer to Jesus' agonizing question from the cross. Why did God the Father forsake his only beloved Son? God forsook Jesus on the cross so that he would never have to forsake us. In that moment, with the full freight and fury of his wrath, God laid upon Jesus the punishment that our sins deserved, so that God would have absolutely no punitive anger left toward us. On the cross, God drained the cup of his wrath dry through the spilling of the perfect and sinless blood of his only begotten son Jesus Christ . . . and he did it *for us*. He could have deputized a hitman to finish us off, but instead he deputized an advocate and defender—the second person of the triune God—to shield and protect us.

I recently heard a Bible teacher say that Jesus did not come to make bad people good, but to make dead people alive. Human sin is not merely a problem to be solved or a hindrance to virtuous living. Apart from Christ we are dead in our sins (Eph. 2:1). This is a multi-billion–dollar debt that is impossible for us to repay. The cross of Jesus Christ, more than any other thing, reveals the insurmountable debt of sin being "surmounted" on our behalf by the Savior himself.

For the wages of sin is death, but the gift of God is eternal life in Christ Jesus our Lord (Rom. 6:23). What could be better than this? What could give us a more compelling reason to do the hard work of forgiving others from the heart, just as we have been forgiven by God in Christ? On this basis, what could stop us from praying, "Forgive us our debts as we forgive our debtors" and *meaning it* from the very bottom and dregs of our tragically indebted yet lovingly redeemed hearts?

The cross not only reveals the gravity of our debt; it also reveals the greater gravity of God's unfailing love for us. How do we know the value of a work of art? How do we recognize its true worth? A work of art is worth what the highest bidder is willing to pay for it.

On the cross, the lifeblood of Jesus was liquidated for your sake. This act also became God's *statement* of your value in Christ and what he was willing to give up in order to redeem, restore, and retain you forever as his child.

You, who have ignored him. You, who have offended and injured him. You, who have insulted him and wished him dead. You, who have contributed to the driving of the nails through his hands and feet.

You.

You are his beloved and blood-bought child. You are his inheritance (Eph. 1:18), his beloved daughter or son (Gal. 4:6), his workmanship (Eph. 2:10), the apple of his eye (Ps. 17:8), the bride with whom he is smitten (Song of Songs, all of it), the crown of his creation made a little less than the angels and with glory and honor (Ps. 8:5), and the joy of his heart worth dying in your stead (Heb. 12:2).

He has not only forgiven you for the wrongs you have done and the injuries you have created for him and for others. He has come to love you with a love that exceeds your greatest imagination and your wildest dreams.

Your God has given you the candlesticks, the light of which will shine on your face until, and infinite days beyond, your final breath.

Forgive, just as God in Christ has forgiven you.

QUESTIONS FOR REFLECTION AND DISCUSSION

1. Name one thing from this chapter that troubled you, inspired you, or both. Why were you impacted in this way?
2. What is your initial response to the biblical and modern-day examples of forgiveness that are featured in this chapter? When you have experienced injury, how has your response resembled these examples? How has your response been different?
3. In one situation, Rachael Denhollander forgave her offender but did not release him from responsibility for the things he had done to her. In another situation, Bishop Myriel forgave his offender and did release him from responsibility. When we are the injured party, how do we determine which of these is the best, most appropriate response?
4. Based on this chapter, identify one way that the Lord might be nudging you toward growth or change. What steps should you take to pursue the change?

EIGHT

We Bless Our Own Betrayers

While living in New York City, a friend and I drove through a neighborhood known for its record-breaking criminal activity. It was not uncommon to turn on the evening news and hear of another break-in, another theft, another violent assault, or another murder taking place in that particular area. Eager to get home to the safety and warmth of our respective Manhattan dwellings, my friend and I were alarmed when a tire on the car went flat. Having no other options, we drove slowly to the nearest service station to see if we could get some help. Knowing the neighborhood could be dangerous, my friend and I both stepped out of the car with a degree of fear. What would happen next? How would we be treated? Would we be scammed, mugged, beaten up, or become the next subjects on the evening news?

To our own shame, my friend and I had our stereotypes of this neighborhood and its residents blown apart by what happened next. Sometimes it's good to remember that what gets reported on the evening news is not the entire story. In fact, what gets reported usually only illuminates a sliver of what goes on in real life.

After we pulled into the station and got out of the car, a man jumped out of the bushes dressed in a plastic trash bag that served as his makeshift raincoat. The man said to us, "Looks like you have a flat tire. I can help with that!" Not wanting to be rude, yet uncertain of what might happen next, my friend and I decided to accept his offer. The young man reached beneath a nearby dumpster, grabbed what appeared to be a toolkit, and within a few minutes the tire was repaired and like new.

Before getting back into the car, we thanked the man from the bushes and asked him how much we owed him. "Oh, you don't owe me anything," he said. "I love helping people. It's what I do." We thanked him sincerely, shook his hand, and asked him what his name was.

"Hitler," the man said. "My name is Hitler. It's nice to meet you both."

Feeling dumbstruck but not wanting to be rude, my friend and I again thanked Hitler before we drove off. As we drove toward our homes, my friend said, "Can you believe that? He said his name was *Hitler.* What kind of parents would give a name like that to their child? What on earth?"

Then we got to talking about Jesus and how this odd incident served as a reminder of how our Savior works. We talked about Abraham, an occasionally cowardly husband whom the Lord made father to all who have faith. We talked about Jacob, a habitual liar whom the Lord made father to the twelve tribes of Israel. We talked about David, an adulterer and murderer whom the Lord commissioned to write half of the psalms and called him a man after God's own heart. We talked about Rahab, a prostitute whom the Lord listed among the faith heroes in Hebrews 11. We talked about Mary Magdalene, a once–demon-possessed woman whom the Lord made the first eyewitness of his resurrection. We talked about Matthew, a crooked thief whom the Lord commissioned to write the first of four gospel accounts. And we talked about Saul of Tarsus, a blasphemer, persecutor, and violent man whom the Lord inspired to write approximately one-third of the New Testament.

Our encounter with Hitler became another reminder to us of Jesus, the Creator-Redeemer who loves to take a bad name and turn it into something good. And it brought us back to the many stories, both ancient and modern, both far away and in our own cities, neighborhoods, homes, and hearts, that prove true the famous statement made by Russian novelist Aleksandr Solzhenitsyn, an outspoken critic of communism. Regarding good, evil, and humanity, he said, "The line dividing good and evil cuts through the heart of every human being."[1]

In this chapter, I would like to examine a key reason why Christians, of all people, ought to be among the most kindhearted, patient, and gentle people in the world—even toward those who betray us. The reason is that that line dividing good and evil, as Solzhenitsyn said, cuts right through *our* hearts as well. Like the German Hitler, apart from Christ we, too, are capable of unspeakable evil and betrayal.

THE JUDAS WITHIN US

Shortly before his death, Jesus prepared and served the annual Passover meal for himself and his twelve disciples in the Upper

Room. As the twelve were reclining at the table eating their meal, Jesus announced to them, "Truly, I say to you, one of you will betray me." When he said these words, Jesus did not single out the disciple Judas as the betrayer or as the infamous "son of perdition" (John 17:12 NKJV). Instead, he used the second-person plural, indicating that any of the twelve could feasibly betray him. Knowing this to be true—knowing that the line dividing good and evil cuts through *every* human heart—none of the disciples responded with an accusation toward another. None said, "Lord, we've all been suspecting this for some time and we're glad you are finally confirming our suspicion. It is Judas, of course! It's so obvious!" Instead, each disciple became sorrowful and introspective, and each one took his turn asking Jesus, "Is it I?" (Mark 14:19).

This "Is it I?" response to the Lord, as opposed to an "It is he!" response, is a key indicator of a healthy, self-aware, non-presumptuous, gentle posture of faith. Sorrow mixed with introspection is, even for the most faithful disciples among us, the most appropriate response when the subject of evil and betrayal is raised. For none of us has measured up to the standard of true faithfulness. And all of us "have sinned and fall short of the glory of God" (Rom. 3:23). The more we realize these truths, the less accusatory we will become toward others, and the gentler we will become as well.

The More Holy We Become, the Less Holy We Feel

Throughout Scripture, we find that the most faithful followers of the Lord—including prophets and apostles—recognize that, in their hearts, they are more like Hitler and Judas than they are like Jesus Christ. Isaiah, one of the greatest prophets Israel has ever known, catches a glimpse of God's glory in the temple and cries out, "Woe is me! For I am lost; for I am a man of unclean lips, and I dwell in the midst of a people of unclean lips; for my eyes have seen the King, the Lord of hosts" (Isa. 6:5). Note that when Isaiah uses the word *unclean*, he does so in reference to his lips. A prophet's gift and calling is to speak the truth, beauty, and glory of God *from* his or her lips. As a herald of heaven whose lips are the most esteemed and sanctified part of him, Isaiah recognizes that even the best, most holy part of him is like a filthy rag when compared to the holiness of God (Isa. 64:6). The angel of the Lord comes to the prophet with a coal from the altar, touches his lips with the coal, and assures him that the Lord has removed and atoned for his guilt (Isa. 6:1–7).

Similarly, after hearing Jesus teach the crowds and witnessing a miraculous catch of fish, Peter could not bear the sight of the Lord—not because of any deficiency he saw in the Lord, but because of the many deficiencies he saw in himself. "Depart from me," Peter said, "for I am a sinful man, O Lord." Jesus replied, "Do not be afraid; from now on you will be catching men" (Luke 5:8, 10).

The apostle Paul, likewise, sensed the line dividing good and evil in his own heart. Ironically, the *more* mature he became in his faith, the *more* virtuous he grew, the *more* active and animated the fruit of the Spirit became in his life, the more aware he also became of the gap between his own sinfulness and the holiness of God. In his early days as a believer, he identified himself as "Paul, an apostle." Later, he became "Paul, the least of the apostles." Then, "Paul, least of all the saints." And finally, toward the end of his life and in one of his last recorded letters to his young protégé and pastor, Timothy, Paul wrote, "The saying is trustworthy and deserving of full acceptance, that Christ Jesus came into the world to save sinners, of whom I am the foremost" (1 Tim. 1:15).

This "Is it I?" level of self-awareness in Paul is also put on display in his letter to the church at Rome, in which he writes, "I find it to be a law that when I want to do right, evil lies close at hand. For I delight in the law of God, in my inner being, but I see in my members another law waging war against the law of my mind and making me captive to the law of sin that dwells in my members. Wretched man that I am! Who will deliver me from this body of death? Thanks be to God through Jesus Christ our Lord!" (Rom. 7:21–25).

Just as Isaiah received assurance from the angel and just as Peter received the same from Jesus, the Holy Spirit impressed the same upon Paul: "There is therefore now no condemnation for those who are in Christ Jesus . . . For I am sure that [nothing] in all creation, will be able to separate us from the love of God in Christ Jesus our Lord" (Rom. 8:1, 38–39).

Throughout history, there have been others who humbly recognized the line dividing good and evil running through their own hearts. Philosopher Søren Kierkegaard speculated that had it been him in Peter's shoes, he, too, would have withdrawn from Christ in self-preservation as Christ began his journey to the cross.[2] In the painting lauded as his first masterpiece, *Judas Returning Thirty Pieces of Silver*, Rembrandt painted his own face as the face of Judas, the betrayer. In his blockbuster film depicting the journey of Jesus Christ to the cross, director Mel Gibson made just one appearance: his was the hand that drove the nails to fasten the body of Christ to the cross.

There, but for the Grace of God, Go I

When we become awakened to the reality of our own sinfulness in contrast to the holiness of God, we find ourselves identifying with Judas rather than holding him in contempt. As the old adage goes, "There, but for the grace of God, go I." Apart from the gentle, forgiving ways of Christ toward us, we are all bound to become sons and daughters of perdition.

Sin and evil are deeper than meets the eye. As Solzhenitsyn wrote, good and evil pass through the human *heart*, which often remains hidden from the outside world. Before it manifests in our behavior, sin and evil first take root beneath the surface, just like a seed underground.

Concerning Judas, one reason why none of the disciples knew he was the betrayer was that, in terms of his behavior and activity, his life looked the same as theirs. Like them, he walked closely with Jesus for approximately three years. Like them, he surely preached the gospel from town to town and saw many come to follow Jesus. Like them, he most certainly performed miracles and cast out demons in Jesus' name. Like them, he would have advocated for the weak and the poor. What made Judas different than the rest was that, in the deeper recesses of his soul, his motives were more twisted than pure. In retrospect, the Gospel writers seem to recognize this fact, as they observe in Judas an unusual and sometimes injurious fixation on money. As the keeper of the treasury, he would often help himself to monies that had been given for the purposes of funding ministry and providing relief to the poor (John 12:6). When he handed Jesus over to the authorities who would lead Jesus to trial and eventually to his death, Judas did so in exchange for thirty pieces of silver (Matt. 26:15).

In his teaching about the so-called "will to power," the German philosopher Friedrich Nietzsche theorized that a key driving force behind why people embrace religion is their own raw, self-serving, personal ambition. According to Nietzsche, religion is not chiefly used as a means to know God, to love our neighbor, or to serve and contribute to the common good, as much as it is to serve ourselves and, as in the case of Judas, to line our own pockets. For some, the motivation is economic. For others, the motivation is to acquire power, recognition, or an advantage that enables us to get what we want.

When I was in college, I began drinking coffee, but not because I liked coffee. In fact, I thought it tasted awful. But I drank it, and drank it gladly, because I was interested in a girl who loved coffee. For me, coffee was not an end in itself, because *by* itself it was not a source of pleasure. Rather, it served as a means toward the end that I really desired—the attention of a particular girl, who happened to like coffee. For Judas, Jesus and ministry had become a means to the end of money. But in retrospect, we realize that Judas never loved or desired Jesus for his own sake. In fact, in the end he was willing to sell out Jesus completely.

If we are to be gracious, gentle people in our current climate, we must recognize that similar tainted and twisted motives reside in us as well. We must pay close attention to Jesus' teaching in the Sermon on the Mount about the deceptive nature of sin. We've got to admit that we, too, can be deceived by sin. Sadly, we can offer prayers to God without a shred of love for God himself, but instead to procure the attention and applause of whoever might be listening to our prayers (Matt. 6:5–6). Likewise, we can abstain from inappropriate sexual activity for our entire lives, but the lust in our hearts reveals an abiding, adulterous intent (Matt. 5:27–30). We can resist the urge to become physically violent toward others, but the hatred and grudges that we carry indicate that, in our hearts, we are murderous (Matt. 5:21–26).

In 2001, the news outlets reported that Andrea Yates, a young mother of five—John, Paul, Luke, Mary, and Noah—became so overwhelmed with the demands of parenting that she drowned all five children in the bathtub of their Houston, Texas, home. Her confirmed mental illness and severe postpartum depression notwithstanding, Yates committed what many would regard as the most heinous form of evil, sending five innocent and helpless children to an early, violent, tragic, and senseless death.

Later that week, we were having dinner with a few friends and the subject of the Yates drowning came up in our conversation. Everyone around the table was grieved and horrified by the story. Then, one of our friends, a mother of young children herself, paused in silence before declaring to the rest of us, "I am certain that given the right set of circumstances, with enough sleep deprivation, mental illness, postpartum hormonal imbalance, and feelings of being overwhelmed, I, too, could have done the same to my children."

For a moment, we all sat silent and slack-jawed at such an honest, troubling confession. The fact that anyone among our friends would say such a thing about her own heart felt frightening, because this woman was the last person on earth that any of us would imagine could commit such an act. But our deeper fear was the fear that her confession stirred in us about our own selves. Her confession pressed us to remember that we, too, have our own vulnerabilities and triggers that might lead us to do something just as inconceivable, just as terrifying, and just as evil as what the young Texas mother did on that one awful and tragic day. For a split second, we all found our own hearts asking the question, "Lord, is it I?"

Indeed, the seed of Judas resides in us all. The seed begins small in the same way that a single HIV virus begins small in an infected human body. Although one strand of HIV is sixty times smaller than a single red blood cell, and although the disease may lie dormant and not manifest openly for many years, it nonetheless has the potential to utterly destroy the entire body. If left untreated, HIV will most certainly multiply and will eventually kill.

Sin is no different than HIV. It may start off seeming small and powerless to us—a brief glance, a click of the mouse, a white lie, ten seconds of gossip, a withholding of the tithe, a moment of neglect, or the nursing of a pet peeve—but over time, if not treated and mortified, the sin in us could develop into full-blown betrayal.

THE GENTLENESS OF JESUS TOWARD BETRAYERS

When we come to the realization that the line of good and evil cuts through our hearts just as it does through the heart of every kind of betrayer, it gives us pause about assuming a holier-than-thou or fiercely oppositional posture in our dealings with others. The more attuned we are to this reality of indwelling sin in *us*—and of the war that goes on inside of *us* between flesh and spirit, the old man and the new creation, good and evil—the more empathetic and gentle and kind we will likely become, even toward those who've done horrendous and unspeakable things. We might even find ourselves starting to feel sorry for, and not merely contempt toward, the likes of Judas and Andrea Yates and our honest friend at the dinner table, as well as others who have discovered their own betrayer-potential through heinous acts, heinous thoughts, or both.

But even—no, especially—those of us who have come to terms with the darkness that is in us can move forward in hope. Why? Because the warm, kindhearted, and gentle response of Jesus toward Isaiah, Peter, Paul, and others is the same response he gives to us, not only when we are at our best, but also when we are at our worst.

He Is Gentle Even Toward Hell-Bound Betrayers

When Jesus announced in the Upper Room that one of his disciples would betray him, he knew precisely the one he was talking about. While it was a mystery to the rest, it was no mystery to him. *Judas* would be the one to betray him into the hands of his enemies, sell him off for thirty coins of silver, and publicly disown him with a terribly ironic and awful kiss (Luke 22:48).

But even so, knowing that Judas would do these things to him for all to see, and knowing that Satan had already entered Judas to lead him in this direction (Luke 22:3), Jesus invited, welcomed, and fed Judas at the meal in the Upper Room. Jesus does not out him in front of the others. There is no shaming or scolding from Jesus toward Judas. He makes no attempt to draw the others in to the drama and sadness and offensiveness of what is about to happen to him at the hands of his betrayer. He makes no attempt to form a mob culture against a common enemy, even though to betray Jesus was to betray the entire group as well. Instead, Jesus covers Judas. In saying, "One of you will betray me" but without revealing the identity of the betrayer, it's as if Jesus is saying to Judas, "I see you, Judas. I know what you are up to. Even so, I am *not* going to humiliate you."

I once heard theologian and New Testament scholar D. A. Carson say that Jesus' restraint here, marked by his refusal to expose or humiliate his soon-to-be betrayer, is Jesus' final act of courtesy and love toward this man in whom Satan himself resides. Similarly, Tim Keller said in a sermon that Jesus did not want to shatter Judas; he wanted to melt him. He didn't want to condemn Judas; he wanted to convict him. Said Keller, "[This is] perfect, thread-the-needle gentleness, the most amazing meshing of justice and sensitivity."[3]

A related, significant detail about Judas's betrayal of Jesus is how our Lord speaks to his betrayer even as Judas is in the very act of committing the betrayal. According to Matthew's gospel, as Judas approaches Jesus to deliver the betrayer's kiss, Jesus says to him, "Friend, do what you came to do" (Matt. 26:50).

Did you catch that? Jesus called his betrayer *friend*.

What on earth?

Mark's gospel helps us understand in part why Jesus would use a term of endearment such as *friend* when speaking to Judas in this awful, dark, and tragic hour of history. During the Upper Room discourse at the final Passover meal before Jesus' journey to the cross, Jesus said of the one who would betray him, "It is one of the twelve, one who is dipping bread into the dish with me. For the Son of Man goes as it is written of him, but woe to that man by whom the Son of Man is betrayed! It would have been better for that man if he had not been born" (Mark 14:20–21).

In scripture, and especially when Jesus is speaking it, the word *woe* is not typically a term of scolding and contempt, but rather is a term compelled by compassion, sadness, longing, and loss. The spirit of the word is also captured as Jesus weeps over the straying and betraying city of Jerusalem, saying, "O Jerusalem, Jerusalem, the city that kills the prophets and stones those who are sent to it! How often would I have gathered your children together as a hen gathers her brood under her wings, and you were not willing! See, your house is left to you desolate" (Matt. 23:37–39).

Judas was not alone in turning on Jesus. In fact, all of the other disciples also betrayed Jesus by failing to support him in Gethsemane and by deserting him as he was arrested and led to the cross. However, after Jesus' crucifixion, they returned to each other and later returned to the risen Lord. The great tragedy in Judas's case is that he never returned—not to the other disciples and not the Lord. Judas was alone in the world with nothing but the haunting thought of what he had done to the most loving, kind, gentle, and virtuous man who ever lived. He concluded the same thing that Jesus had—that it would have been better for the one who would betray Jesus to have not been born. Then, in his darkest and most isolated hour, Judas made his final exit from his tragic life by slipping a noose over his own neck and hanging himself from a tree (Matt. 27:1–10).

There was no joy in heaven when Judas the betrayer made his final exit. Instead, there was much grief in the heart of God. "As I live, declares the Lord God, I have no pleasure in the death of the wicked, but that the wicked turn from his way and live; turn back, turn back from your evil ways, for why will you die, O house of Israel?" (Ezek. 33:11).

He Turns in Love Toward Every Betrayer Who Turns Toward Him

As I have already mentioned, Judas was not the only disciple who betrayed Jesus. The Gospel accounts tell us that while Jesus was on his way to the cross, *all* of the disciples deserted him and fled (Mark 14:50). This included the zealous Peter, who had only hours before sworn complete loyalty to Jesus, come hell or high water, even if it led him to a certain death (Luke 22:33). But like many of us, Peter's passionate resolve to follow Jesus with complete devotion withered as soon as he realized how costly it would be for him to remain true to Jesus through thick and thin.

The tide of popular opinion had turned full bore against Jesus. Following Judas's betrayal, the authorities seized Jesus and brought him to trial, which resulted in a brutal bloodbath at the hands of Roman soldiers whose favorite pastime was to inflict lingering, excruciating pain upon their subjects. Jesus would die a slow death while hanging naked on a cross, utterly humiliated in the eyes of God and men. Peter, realizing that siding with Jesus would mean dying with him in similar fashion, decided to go dark. Instead of courageously following Jesus in loyalty to the bitter end, Peter retreated into self-preservation, so as to keep a safe distance from having to bear the costs of love and true discipleship. Instead of denying himself, taking up his cross, and following Jesus, Peter instead denied Jesus, took up his comforts, and followed the crowds. When suspected by local residents and passers-by of being a friend of Jesus, Peter categorically denied it—three times a betrayer—to save his own hide. Then, like a dog with its tail tucked beneath its backside, Peter sat quietly watching as Jesus was led away to the cross. As he sat, he warmed himself at a fire stoked by people who hated Jesus. Then, as he walked away to bear his cross alone, Jesus gave Peter a split second of eye contact. That was all it took for Peter to retreat into shame and isolation, just as Judas had. Having realized the true potential of his own heart to do things he once thought himself incapable of doing—utterly and thrice betraying the One who loved him and gave himself for him—Peter found a quiet spot and wept bitterly (Luke 22:54–62).

Before we rush to the next part of Peter's story, which is so much more hopeful than the tragic end of Judas's story, we need to name a reality that exists not only in our own culture and communities but in our own hearts as well. We, too, are susceptible to warming ourselves at a fire created by the enemies of Jesus, surrendering our wills and ways to the tide of popular opinion. We, too, protect ourselves from having to take up crosses that Jesus—whose will and ways are counterculture to every culture—is calling us to carry in such a time as ours.

In our modern context, a growing number of people who identify as Christian can, like Peter, allow themselves to become disciples of popular opinion as opposed to living as cross-bearing, countercultural disciples of Jesus. This is especially true in areas where staying true to Jesus feels threatening socially, vocationally, politically, or otherwise. When blending in to popular opinion and staying on good terms with a world that does not love Jesus becomes priority, these Christians will eventually find themselves in a world of compromise.

On the one hand, the Peters of today will continue offering an enthusiastic thumbs-up to biblical teachings that remain in accord with popular thought. God is love . . . *thumbs-up!* God is forgiving . . . *thumbs-up!* God loves diversity, valuing people from every nation and tribe and tongue . . . *thumbs-up!* God is concerned with social action, caring for the poor, lifting up the weak, healing the sick, relieving those in pain, protecting the unborn, and providing sanctuary for the alien and stranger and refugee . . . *thumbs-up!*

On the other hand, the same people will, over time, find themselves offering a "thumbs-down" to other biblical truths that Jesus affirmed, defended, and taught. *Thumbs-down* to what

Jesus taught about sex, gender, and marriage! *Thumbs-down* to the things he said about hell and judgment! *Thumbs-down* to what he said about being the way, the truth, and the life, and that no one comes to the Father except through him! *Thumbs-down* on how Jesus referred to himself as *the* truth, thus declaring null and void any version of "your truth" and "my truth" that is not in accord with what he says is the truth.

We must admit that we are susceptible to failing Jesus in the same way that Peter betrayed him. When popular opinion, or the opinion of our closest friends or family members or bosses or colleagues or neighbors, is found to be out of sorts with what Jesus said is true, noble, lovely, excellent, and praiseworthy—we, like Peter, can just as easily go dark, betray our Lord, and warm ourselves at a fire kindled by a world that loves neither Jesus nor us. In the same way that his own act of betrayal caused Peter to weep bitterly, our own betrayals will lead us into grief if the Spirit of God resides in us. Like Peter, our hearts will be struck with Spirit-filled sorrow over the things we've thought, said, and done. This undoing is God's gracious way of calling us to turn back to him and return home.

I am still haunted by something I did in high school. At the time, I was a deeply insecure teenage boy trying to navigate a world filled with sharks and minnows, queen bees and wannabes, jocks and nerds, in-crowds and out-crowds, and all the rest that defines the tumultuous years of high school. Afraid of rejection and desperate to be liked, I decided that I would try the class clown option. In an effort to make my homeroom classmates laugh, I singled out a girl in the room and said loudly in her direction, "Hey, _____, you are so ugly!" The room filled with laughter. Then, wanting to add to the momentum of this moment, I singled out a boy in the room and said loudly in his direction, "Hey, _____, you are so dumb!" Again, the room filled with laughter.

As I write this, I am fifty-one years old, and to this day I remain haunted by how easy it was for me to numb my own social pain and fear by adding to the social pain and fear of these two beautiful, fearfully and wonderfully made, image-bearing souls.

Do you have any such memories of your own? If you could rewind the clock and reverse something that you thought, said, or did—would you undo a time you betrayed another person, and in so doing betrayed the God in whose likeness they were created? Are you still haunted by the memory? Is there a part of you that, deep in the recesses of your soul, continues to "weep bitterly" over this hurtful experience? What's more, does your soul weep bitterly over the realization that you are just as capable now as you were then of being a betrayer?

"And Peter"

In the midst of such memories and realizations, we can take heart, just as Peter was able to take heart. Because after Jesus was crucified and buried for three days he rose victorious from the grave in triumph over sin and death. When the women arrived at the tomb and discovered that Jesus was alive again, the Lord paid them a visit and said to them, "Do not be alarmed . . . But go, tell his disciples *and Peter* that [Jesus] is going before you to Galilee. There you will see him, just as he told you" (Mark 16:6–7, emphasis mine).

This was the first word that Peter the betrayer heard from Jesus. Whereas Jesus did *not* single Judas out in the Upper Room in order to humiliate him, Jesus *did* single Peter out after his resurrection in order to reassure and restore him. "I am singling you out, Peter, because more than anyone else you are feeling a distance from me, as if you've blown it completely, as if you've reached a point of no return with me. You have not. You will see me, Peter, just as I told you. I am coming to you."

In John's account of the same event, we are told that Jesus speaks additional words of affirmation, warmth, and gentleness. He says to the women at the tomb, "Go to my brothers and say to them, 'I am ascending to my Father and your Father, to my God and your God'" (John 20:17). Did you hear that? He calls those who have betrayed and deserted him his brothers. He says that they share the same Father in heaven, and that his God is still their God. *They are family, and nothing will ever be able to change that.* Jesus takes a bad name, Betrayer, and turns it into something else—something loving, gracious, and gentle—the Betrayer in each of the disciples, the Betrayer in Peter, has been given the new name of Brother.

Later, Jesus is with his disciples and turns to Peter, asking him three times, "Peter, do you love me?" Each time, Peter responds with a resounding yes. Then the Lord, filled with kindness and affection toward Peter, tells Peter that he wants him to feed his sheep and tend to his lambs. "Not only are you my brother, Peter, but from this point forward you are also the keeper of all my brothers. That is how highly I esteem you, my good friend. That is how much I believe in you, and in what my Father and your Father, my God and your God, intends to do through you."

Peter embraced his new name. This Betrayer-turned-Brother became a man of unshakable courage—a true rock who would exhibit courageous and loving leadership in the early church and die as a martyr for Jesus' sake. In his *Works of Love,* Søren Kierkegaard depicts the transformation of Peter in this way:

> Christ's love for Peter was so boundless that in loving Peter he accomplished loving the person one sees. He did not say, "Peter must change first and become another man before I can love him again." No, just the opposite, he said, "Peter is Peter, and I love him; love, if anything, will help him to become another man." Therefore he did not break off the friendship in order perhaps to renew it again when Peter had become another man. No, he preserved the friendship unchanged and in this very way helped Peter to become another man. Do you think that Peter would have been won again without this faithful friendship of Christ?[4]

This "faithful friendship" about which Kierkegaard wrote is the gentleness of Christ, which warms us so much better than the fires kindled by those who do not love Christ. And it is the warmth of his gentleness alone that can turn us into the best, most courageous, most life-giving, and most earth-shaking versions of ourselves.

So then, which fire shall we choose?

QUESTIONS FOR REFLECTION AND DISCUSSION

1. Name one thing from this chapter that troubled you, inspired you, or both. Why were you impacted in this way?
2. Which response from Jesus to his two fallen disciples is more compelling to you? Is it when he calls Judas "friend," or is it when he says "and Peter" to the women? Why do you answer in the way that you do?

3. As I've pointed out, every Christian has inside him an "inner Jesus" as well as an "inner Judas." Do you think it is important to be aware of an "inner Jesus?" Of an "inner Judas?" Why or why not?
4. Based on this chapter, identify one way that the Lord might be nudging you toward growth or change. What steps should you take to pursue the change?

Moving Forward

Shortly after Slate *magazine released its* series of essays about outrage (see the introduction), journalist Emma Green published a similar piece entitled "Taming Christian Rage."[1]

Yes, you read correctly.

Christian rage.

According to her and too many others, those who say they follow Christ can be as much a part of the problem as they are a part of the solution. Christians can wield excessively partisan politics, wave views and attitudes that are shaped more by cable news than by Scripture, exert a polarizing culture war mentality, show lack of impulse control on social media, and hold a judgmental, critical spirit toward *others* and the sins *out there.* How disturbing it is when we are reluctant to humbly address the rage that resides in our own Christian communities, homes, and hearts.

As one secular journalist quipped, "The trouble with born-again Christians is that they are an even bigger pain the second time around."[2]

Wherever this is true of us, Jesus stands against our efforts.

Wherever this is true of us, the Holy Spirit is grieved.

Wherever this is true of us, the Father desires more *from* us and better *for* us.

As I hope the preceding chapters have shown, Jesus calls his followers to something better and more life-giving than oppositional postures. Armed with a gentle answer, modeled and provided by our gentle Savior himself, it is time we got about the business of mending our fractured world with a presence that is less combative and more gentle and kind. The flourishing of our witness depends on it, and the good name of our Savior is worthy of it.

Days before his arrest, Jesus looked across the city of Jerusalem, knowing that its people and leaders would soon call for his execution. He knew they would sneer and gloat as they watched him die a slow, shameful death. He would be overwhelmed by isolation, injury, and betrayal that cut deeper than words can describe. Instead of harboring ill will toward them, he wept with compassion over the city (Matt. 23:37; Luke 19:41).

And then on the night of his betrayal, when the high priest approached Jesus to arrest and crucify him, the disciple Simon Peter quickly pulled out his sword and severed the ear of Malchus, one of the high priest's servants. Malchus was a threat to Jesus, and Simon Peter instinctively wanted to block the attack. Jesus, however, did not support Simon Peter's retaliatory behavior. Instead, he rebuked him, saying, "Put your sword into its sheath; shall I not drink the cup that the Father has given me?" (John 18:11). Then, Jesus gently touched his enemy, stopped the bleeding, and healed him completely (Luke 22:47–53).

Jesus relinquishes his justifiable outrage and advances his gentleness toward us as well. Jesus saved us, not because of righteous things we have done, but because of his mercy (Titus 3:4–6).

God demonstrates his love toward us in that while we were *still* sinners—while we were still opposed to him, hostile toward him, insulting him, and wishing him dead—Christ died for us (Rom. 5:8).

When the hatred of humanity was directed toward Jesus, he had every right to retaliate. He could have responded to the entire human race with outrage and rejection and injury. He could have sliced off our ears, called fire down on us from heaven, and subjected us to the terrors of judgment. But he didn't do any of this. Instead, he left his sword in its sheath and counteracted our hostility with a gentle answer.

The gentle answer that comes from Jesus defuses wrath instead of fanning its flame (Prov. 15:1). Within it resides the power to subdue fruitless arguments, break vicious cycles, turn enemies into friends, end wars, and change history. Within it resides the power of a future where wolves dwell in harmony with lambs, leopards with young goats, and lions with fattened cows (Isa. 11:6).

Animals will cease devouring each other, and so will people. Jews will dwell in harmony with Gentiles, blacks with whites, the rich with the poor, political liberals with political conservatives, and those who have been injured with the people who have injured them. Within the gentle answer resides the power for stories to continue emerging where one person will say of another, "He who used to persecute us is now preaching the faith he once tried to destroy" (Gal. 1:23).

Hope for this kind of world and future has a prerequisite. Before our hearts can be warmed by the idea of such radical reconciliation and peace, they must first be melted and softened. We must become settled in the truth that whatever Jesus asks *from* us, he has already done *for* us. Only then can we grow thicker skin, do anger well, receive criticism graciously, forgive all the way, bless our own betrayers, befriend our fellow sinners, resist our inner moralist, disarm guarded postures, and anything else of the sort. At the cross of Calvary, he confronted our violence with his nonviolence, our hostility with his forgiveness, and our wrath with his gentle answer.

It is *never* our repentance that causes God to be kind to us.

It is *only* God's kindness that causes us to repent (Rom. 2:4).

Because Jesus Christ has instituted and sealed this love relationship with us, his former enemies, we are able to navigate the world in the same manner as our Lord. Only when we embody a bold gentleness will our outraged world begin to notice that we are distinctly *his* disciples (John 17:1–26). When we do this, and only when we do this, an outraged world stops identifying Christians as a core part of the problem, and instead begins believing that Christians are a most necessary part of the solution.

In his exposition of the Sermon on the Mount, Dr. Martyn Lloyd-Jones says that Christians are a light *to* the world only to the degree that they stand out as different *from* the world. The world does not thirst for a religious imitation of its often-outraged self. Instead, the world thirsts for a different kind of neighbor, the kind that embodies in a most life-giving, countercultural fashion the following "Peace Prayer" from Saint Francis.

May we learn not only to recite these words but to live them. Because gentle talk, if not accompanied by a gentle walk, will get us nowhere.

> Lord, make me an instrument of your peace.
> Where there is hatred, let me bring love.

Where there is offense, let me bring pardon.
Where there is discord, let me bring union.
Where there is error, let me bring truth.
Where there is doubt, let me bring faith.
Where there is despair, let me bring hope.
Where there is darkness, let me bring your light.
Where there is sadness, let me bring joy.
O Master, let me not seek as much
to be consoled as to console,
to be understood as to understand,
to be loved as to love,
for it is in giving that one receives,
it is in self-forgetting that one finds,
it is in pardoning that one is pardoned,
it is in dying that one is raised to eternal life.

Acknowledgments

To Wes Yoder, it's really been fun getting to work on this stuff with you. And we're just getting started. You are an even better friend than you are an agent—and you're really great at both.

To Webb Younce and HarperCollins Christian, thanks for believing in my work and for wanting to put it out there, in hopes that it might grow some wings and help some people along the way.

To Darryl and Ann Voskamp, I've wanted to quit writing ever since I started doing it. You have encouraged me, one project after the next, to keep going. Thank you for that and thank you for being you. You speak words that make souls stronger. You put courage into others, especially me.

To the elders at Christ Presbyterian Church in Nashville, thanks for letting me do this. Truly.

To Russ Ramsey, my pastoral and writing colleague and friend. Thanks for persuading me to use exclamation points sparingly (!). Because substance, not flash, is what ultimately changes things.

To Abby and Ellie, you are no longer in the nest, but are still and will always be fully in our hearts. We love you and couldn't be prouder of you. Come home often.

To Patti, no project like this is my project, it's *our* project. You've been the first editor for every chapter I've ever written, which I'm certain makes the other, later editors very happy. You are an outstanding communicator in your own right, and an even more outstanding servant and friend and mom and wife. Thanks for choosing to see me in the same way that our dog sees me, even though you know better.

Notes

Introduction

1. John Perkins, *Let Justice Roll Down* (Grand Rapids: Baker, 1976), Kindle edition.
2. Staff, "The Year of Outrage," *Slate*, December 17, 2014, www.slate.com/articles/life/culturebox/2014/12/the_year_of_outrage_2014_everything_you_were_angry_about_on_social_media.html.
3. Dino-Ray Ramos, "Texas Congressman-Elect Dan Crenshaw Reaches Out to SNL's Pete Davidson After Troubling Instagram Post," *Deadline*, December 18, 2018, deadline.com/2018/12/dan-crenshaw-pete-davidson-snl-saturday-night-live-instagram-post-1202522842/.

Chapter 1: He Befriends the Sinner in Us

1. Christopher Hibbert, *Disraeli: The Victorian Dandy Who Became Prime Minister* (London: Samuel French Ltd., 1958), 336.
2. It is important to acknowledge that viewing a sex offender in light of gospel truth does *not* mean we don't use wisdom and seek to establish healthy, safe parameters—e.g., George may need accountability, be ruled out from serving in the nursery, and so on. As in all such instances, considerations such as safety, well-being, and the consequences of past actions must be taken into account.
3. I once heard Tim Keller use this phrase in a sermon to describe the likes of Zacchaeus.
4. Francis Maxwell, "Exposing America's Biggest Hypocrites:

Evangelical Christians," *Huffington Post*, November 25, 2017, www.huffingtonpost.com/entry/exposing-americas-biggest-hypocrites-evangelical_us_5a184f0ee4b068a3ca6df7ad.

5. Leo Tolstoy and R. F. Christian, *Tolstoy's Letters*, vol.2 (Oxford: Athalone Press, 1978), 362–63.
6. Corrie ten Boom, *Tramp for the Lord* (Berkley: Jove Books, 1978), 53–55.
7. I first heard this phrase from Tim Keller, who used it in a sermon.

Chapter 2: He Reforms the Pharisee in Us

1. C. S. Lewis, *Reflections on the Psalms* (San Diego: Harcourt, 1958), 95–96.
2. Barna Group, "Almost Half of Practicing Christian Millennials Say Evangelism Is Wrong," Barna Research, February 5, 2019, www.barna.com/research/millennials-oppose-evangelism/.
3. Elizabeth Baker, "I Don't Want to Call Myself a Christian Anymore," *Huffington Post*, July 13, 2017, www.huffingtonpost.com/entry/i-dont-want-to-call-myself-a-christian-anymore_us_596199c5e4b085e766b51360.
4. Baker, "I Don't Want to Call Myself a Christian Anymore."
5. Baker, "I Don't Want to Call Myself a Christian Anymore."
6. *Saved!*, directed by Brian Dannelly (Los Angeles: United Artists, 2004), DVD.
7. I was first introduced to this confession by Rev. Ray Ortlund, who adapted it from an earlier version by Rev. James Montgomery Boice.
8. *Amadeus*, directed by Milos Forman (Berkeley, CA: Saul Zaentz Company, 1984), VHS.
9. Nicholas Kristof, "A Confession of Liberal Intolerance," *New York Times*, May 7, 2016, www.nytimes.com/2016/05/08/opinion/sunday/a-confession-of-liberal-intolerance.html.
10. Kristof, "A Confession of Liberal Intolerance."

Chapter 3: He Disarms the Cynic in Us

1. The name has been changed to protect confidentiality.

2. *Forrest Gump*, directed by Robert Zemeckis (New York: Wendy Finerman Productions, 1994), DVD.
3. Friedrich Nietzsche, *Thus Spoke Zarathustra: A Book for Everyone and Nobody* (Cary: Oxford University Press, 2009), xviii.
4. "Pilate and Christ," words by Tim Rice, music by Andrew Lloyd Webber, from *Jesus Christ Superstar*, 1970.
5. Jean-Paul Sartre, *No Exit: A Play in One Act* (London: Samuel French Ltd., 1958).
6. Cormac McCarthy, *No Country for Old Men* (New York: Vintage, 2006), 267.
7. Joseph Shapiro, "Amish Forgive School Shooter, Struggle with Grief," *NPR*, October 2, 2007, www.npr.org/templates/story/story.php?storyId=14900930.
8. Martin Luther King Jr., *Where Do We Go from Here: Chaos or Community?* (Boston: Beacon Press, 2010), 62–63.

Chapter 4: We Grow Thicker Skin

1. The Declaration of Independence, www.ushistory.org/declaration/document/index.html.
2. Joshua Berlinger, "Detention of 100 Christians Raises Concerns About Religious Crackdown in China," *CNN*, December 17, 2018, www.cnn.com/2018/12/15/asia/wang-yi-early-rain-church-intl/index.html.
3. Wang Yi, "My Declaration of Faithful Disobedience—Pastor Wang Yi (English Translation)," Steve Childers, December 18, 2018, www.stevechilders.org/5862–2-2/.
4. Tertullian, *Apologeticus*, chapter 50.
5. Brian, "10 Dangerous Myths About the Persecuted Church," *Open Doors*, April 24, 2017, www.opendoorsusa.org/christian-persecution/stories/10-dangerous-myths-about-the-persecuted-church/.
6. For example, see Ps. 82:3–4; Prov. 14:31; 31:8–9; Isa. 1:17; 58:6–7; Luke 14:14; Gal. 2:10.
7. Elie Wiesel, "Nobel Prize Speech," Elie Wiesel Foundation for

Humanity, December 10, 1986, eliewieselfoundation.org /elie-wiesel/nobelprizespeech/.

8. Tom Wright, *Matthew for Everyone, Part 1: Chapters 1–15* (Louisville, KY: Westminster John Knox Press, 2004), Logos Bible Software edition.
9. Dietrich Bonhoeffer, *The Cost of Discipleship* (New York: Touchstone, 1995), 90.
10. Associated Press, "Dr. Koop Warns of Spread of AIDS," *New York Times*, January 20, 1987, www.nytimes.com/1987/01/20/us /dr-koop-warns-of-spread-of-aids.html.
11. Associated Press, "Dr. Koop Warns of Spread of AIDS."
12. Bonhoeffer, *Cost of Discipleship*, 127.
13. John Stott, *The Beatitudes: Developing Christian Character* (Downers Grove, IL: IVP Connect, 1998), 54.
14. As quoted in Kent Hughes, *Liberating Ministry from the Success Syndrome* (Wheaton: Tyndale House, 1987), 127.
15. Stott, *Beatitudes*.
16. C. S. Lewis, *The Great Divorce* (New York: HarperOne, 1973), Kindle edition.
17. *Schindler's List*, directed by Steven Spielberg (Universal City, CA: Amblin Entertainment, 1993), DVD.
18. CNN, "Falwell Apologizes to Gays, Feminists, Lesbians," *CNN*, September 14, 2001, http://www.cnn.com/2001/US/09/14/Falwell. apology/.
19. Larry Flynt, "Larry Flynt: My Friend, Jerry Falwell," *Los Angeles Times*, May 20, 2007, www.latimes.com/la-op-flynt20may20 -story.html.

Chapter 5: We Do Anger Well

1. Anne Lamott, *Traveling Mercies* (New York: Pantheon, 1999), Kindle edition.
2. Frederick Buechner, *Wishful Thinking: A Theological ABC* (New York: Harper & Row, 1973), 2.
3. Letitia Rowlands, "US School Provides Worst Bullying Advice

Ever," *Essentialkids*, April 17, 2014, www.essentialkids.com .au/development-advice/behaviour-discipline/us-school -provides-worst-bullying-advice-ever-20140417–36u4k#utm _source=FD&utm_medium=lifeandstylepuff&utm_campaign =bully.

4. Martin Luther King Jr., "Letter from a Birmingham Jail (16 Apr. 1963)," African Studies Center, University of Pennsylvania, www .africa.upenn.edu/Articles_Gen/Letter_Birmingham.html.
5. King, "Birmingham Jail."
6. Martin Luther King Jr., "Martin Luther King Jr. Acceptance Speech (10 Dec. 1964)," Nobel Prize, www.nobelprize.org/prizes /peace/1964/king/acceptance-speech/.
7. "Mother Teresa Speaks Against Abortion at 1994 National Prayer Breakfast (3 Feb. 1994)," transcription, C-SPAN, www.c-span.org /video/?c4618931/mother-teresa-speaks-abortion-1994-national -prayer-breakfast.
8. "Mother Teresa," C-SPAN.
9. C. S. Lewis, *Mere Christianity* (New York: HarperOne, 2001), 37–38.
10. Rebecca Manley Pippert, *Hope Has Its Reasons* (Downers Grove, IL: InterVarsity Press, 2001), 100–101.
11. Kristin Wong, "George Carlin Was Right: Other Drivers Are 'Idiots' and 'Maniacs,'" CNBC News, October 23, 2015, https://www.cnbc.com/2015/10/23/george-carlin-was-right -other-drivers-are-idiots-and-maniacs.html.
12. John Owen, *The Mortification of Sin* (Edinburgh: Banner of Truth, 2004), 17.
13. Jay Sklar, "How to Repent of Slander in a Digital Age," Covenant Theological Seminary, www.covenantseminary.edu/theology /how-to-repent-of-slander-in-a-digital-age/.

Chapter 6: We Receive Criticism Graciously

1. Charles Haddon Spurgeon, *Faith in All Its Splendor* (Lafayette, IN: Sovereign Grace Publishers, 2001), 73.

2. Dietrich Bonhoeffer, *Life Together* (New York: Harper & Row, 1954), Kindle edition.
3. Charles Swindoll, *The Strength of an Exacting Passion* (Nashville: W Publishing Group, 1992), 72.
4. Flemming Rose, "Safe Spaces on College Campuses Are Creating Intolerant Students," Cato Institute, March 30, 2017, www.cato.org/publications/commentary/safe-spaces-college-campuses-are-creating-intolerant-students.
5. Kingsley Martin, "Winston Churchill Interviewed in 1939: 'The British People Would Rather Go Down Fighting,'" *New Stateman America*, January 6, 2014, www.newstatesman.com/archive/2013/12/british-people-would-rather-go-down-fighting.
6. Tim Keller (@timkellernyc), on Twitter, June 16, 2016, twitter.com/timkellernyc/status/743444060577345536.
7. Timothy Keller, "How Do You Take Criticism of Your Views?," Timothy Keller (blog), December 16, 2009, https://timothykeller.com/blog/2009/12/16/how-do-you-take-criticism-of-your-views.
8. Fortune Editors, "The World's 50 Greatest Leaders," *Fortune*, April 19, 2018, http://fortune.com/longform/worlds-greatest-leaders-2018/.
9. Celeste Kennel-Shank, "Princeton Seminary Cancels Award to Tim Keller, but Not His Lecture," *Christian Century*, April 4, 2017, www.christiancentury.org/article/princeton-seminary-cancels-award-tim-keller-not-his-lecture.
10. Katherine Leary Alsdorf, "OpEd: Tim Keller Hired Women in Leadership," Journey Through NYC Religions, March 29, 2017, www.nycreligion.info/oped-tim-keller-put-charge-train-men-women-leadership/.

Chapter 7: We Forgive All the Way

1. Niall McCarthy, "America's Most & Least Trusted Professions," *Forbes*, January 11, 2019, www.forbes.com/sites/niallmccarthy

/2019/01/11/americas-most-least-trusted-professions
-infographic/#7d864dcf7e94.

2. Dan Allender, "Look Your Anger in the Face," Christian Psych, www.christianpsych.org/wp_scp/wp-content/uploads/look-your -anger-in-the-face-allender.pdf.
3. Dan Allender, *Bold Love* (Colorado Springs: NavPress, 1992), 16–30.
4. C. S. Lewis, *Mere Christianity* (New York: HarperOne, 2015), Kindle edition.
5. Dallas Willard, *The Divine Conspiracy* (New York: Harper, 1998), 153.
6. Emily Shapiro, "Charleston Victim's Mother Tells Dylann Roof 'I Forgive You' as He's Sentenced to Death," *ABC News*, January 11, 2017, abcnews.go.com/US/charleston-victims-mother-tells -dylann-roof-forgive/story?id=44704096.
7. Miroslav Volf, *Exclusion and Embrace* (Nashville: Abingdon Press, 1996), Kindle edition.
8. Rachael Denhollander, "Read Rachael Denhollander's Full Victim Impact Statement about Larry Nassar," *CNN*, January 30, 2018, www.cnn.com/2018/01/24/us/rachael-denhollander-full -statement/index.html.
9. Booker T. Washington, *Up from Slavery* (1901), chapter 11.
10. Victor Hugo, *Les Miserables* (New York: Modern Library, 1992), 1,200.
11. Tom Wright, *Matthew for Everyone*, part 2 (Louisville: Westminster John Knox Press, 2004), Logos edition.
12. Volf, *Exclusion and Embrace*, #.

Chapter 8: We Bless Our Own Betrayers

1. Aleksandr Solzhenitsyn, *The Gulag Archipelago* (New York: Harper & Row, 1973), Kindle edition.
2. Søren Kierkegaard, *The Sickness Unto Death* (United Kingdom: A & D Publishing, 2018), Kindle edition.
3. Timothy Keller, "The Betrayers," sermon, January 28, 2007, Redeemer Presbyterian Church, New York, NY.

4. Søren Kierkegaard, *Works of Love* (Princeton, NJ: Princeton University Press, 1995), 172.

Moving Forward

1. Emma Green, "Taming Christian Rage," *Atlantic*, January 6, 2015, www.theatlantic.com/politics/archive/2015/01/taming-christian-culture-war-rage/383908/.
2. Herb Caen, *San Francisco Chronicle*, July 20, 1981.

About the Author

Scott Sauls serves as senior pastor of Christ Presbyterian Church, a multisite church in Nashville, Tennessee (christpres.org). Scott has been married to Patti since 1995, and is dad to Abby and Ellie. Prior to Nashville, Scott was a lead and preaching pastor at New York City's Redeemer Presbyterian Church, planted churches in Kansas City and St. Louis, and taught homiletics (preaching) at Covenant Theological Seminary. Formative experiences have included being an athlete, living in a global city, and suffering through a season of anxiety and depression. A self-described "accidental author," Scott has released four books prior to this one. Influential voices in Scott's life include Tim Keller, C. S. Lewis, Jonathan Edwards, Soong-Chan Rah, Johnny Cash, Joni Eareckson Tada, Paul Tripp, Ann Voskamp, Martin Luther King Jr., Dorothy Sayers, and N. T. Wright. In his free time, you might find Scott relaxing with people or a book, strumming his Gibson guitar, hiking, enjoying live music, or cheering on the St. Louis Cardinals and North Carolina Tar Heels.

Scott blogs weekly at scottsauls.com and has also authored *Jesus Outside the Lines, Befriend, From Weakness to Strength,* and *Irresistible Faith*. You can find him on Twitter and Instagram (@scottsauls) and Facebook (facebook.com/scott.sauls.7).